Civil Rights

Civil Rights

Other books in the Current Controversies series:

Civil Rights

Karen F. Balkin, *Book Editor*

Bruce Glassman, *Vice President*
Bonnie Szumski, *Publisher*
Scott Barbour, *Managing Editor*
Helen Cothran, *Senior Editor*

CURRENT CONTROVERSIES

GREENHAVEN
PRESS®

THOMSON
™
GALE

San Diego • Detroit • New York • San Francisco • Cleveland
New Haven, Conn. • Waterville, Maine • London • Munich

THOMSON

━━━━━━━✴━━━━━━━ ™

GALE

© 2004 by Greenhaven Press. Greenhaven Press is an imprint of The Gale Group, Inc., a division of Thomson Learning, Inc.

Greenhaven® and Thomson Learning™ are trademarks used herein under license.

For more information, contact
Greenhaven Press
27500 Drake Rd.
Farmington Hills, MI 48331-3535
Or you can visit our Internet site at http://www.gale.com

LIBRARY OF CONGRESS CATALOGING-IN-PUBLICATION DATA
Civil rights / Karen F. Balkin, book editor.
p. cm. — (Current controversies)
Includes bibliographical references and index.
ISBN 0-7377-1178-7 (lib. : alk. paper) — ISBN 0-7377-1177-9 (pbk. : alk. paper)
1. Minorities—Civil rights—United States. 2. Affirmative action programs— United States. 3. Terrorism—United States—Prevention. 4. National security— Law and legislation—United States. I. Balkin, Karen F., 1949– . II. Series.
JC599.U5C5618 2004
323.173—dc22   2003060822

Printed in the United States of America

Contents

Chapter 2: Should Civil Rights Protections Be Increased?

Yes: Increased Civil Rights Protection Is Necessary

No: Antiterrorist Measures Do Not Threaten Civil Rights

Foreword

By definition, controversies are "discussions of questions in which opposing opinions clash" (Webster's Twentieth Century Dictionary Unabridged). Few would deny that controversies are a pervasive part of the human condition and exist on virtually every level of human enterprise. Controversies transpire between individuals and among groups, within nations and between nations. Controversies supply the grist necessary for progress by providing challenges and challengers to the status quo. They also create atmospheres where strife and warfare can flourish. A world without controversies would be a peaceful world; but it also would be, by and large, static and prosaic.

The Series' Purpose

The purpose of the Current Controversies series is to explore many of the social, political, and economic controversies dominating the national and international scenes today. Titles selected for inclusion in the series are highly focused and specific. For example, from the larger category of criminal justice, Current Controversies deals with specific topics such as police brutality, gun control, white collar crime, and others. The debates in Current Controversies also are presented in a useful, timeless fashion. Articles and book excerpts included in each title are selected if they contribute valuable, long-range ideas to the overall debate. And wherever possible, current information is enhanced with historical documents and other relevant materials. Thus, while individual titles are current in focus, every effort is made to ensure that they will not become quickly outdated. Books in the Current Controversies series will remain important resources for librarians, teachers, and students for many years.

In addition to keeping the titles focused and specific, great care is taken in the editorial format of each book in the series. Book introductions and chapter prefaces are offered to provide background material for readers. Chapters are organized around several key questions that are answered with diverse opinions representing all points on the political spectrum. Materials in each chapter include opinions in which authors clearly disagree as well as alternative opinions in which authors may agree on a broader issue but disagree on the possible solutions. In this way, the content of each volume in Current Controversies mirrors the mosaic of opinions encountered in society. Readers will quickly realize that there are many viable answers to these complex issues. By questioning each author's conclusions, students and casual readers can begin to develop the critical thinking skills so important to evaluating opinionated material.

Current Controversies is also ideal for controlled research. Each anthology in the series is composed of primary sources taken from a wide gamut of informational categories including periodicals, newspapers, books, United States and foreign government documents, and the publications of private and public organizations. Readers will find factual support for reports, debates, and research papers covering all areas of important issues. In addition, an annotated table of contents, an index, a book and periodical bibliography, and a list of organizations to contact are included in each book to expedite further research.

Perhaps more than ever before in history, people are confronted with diverse and contradictory information. During the Persian Gulf War, for example, the public was not only treated to minute-to-minute coverage of the war, it was also inundated with critiques of the coverage and countless analyses of the factors motivating U.S. involvement. Being able to sort through the plethora of opinions accompanying today's major issues, and to draw one's own conclusions, can be a complicated and frustrating struggle. It is the editors' hope that Current Controversies will help readers with this struggle.

Greenhaven Press anthologies primarily consist of previously published material taken from a variety of sources, including periodicals, books, scholarly journals, newspapers, government documents, and position papers from private and public organizations. These original sources are often edited for length and to ensure their accessibility for a young adult audience. The anthology editors also change the original titles of these works in order to clearly present the main thesis of each viewpoint and to explicitly indicate the opinion presented in the viewpoint. These alterations are made in consideration of both the reading and comprehension levels of a young adult audience. Every effort is made to ensure that Greenhaven Press accurately reflects the original intent of the authors included in this anthology.

"While employment discrimination based on race, ethnicity, and gender has diminished substantially in response to legislative and societal changes, prejudice against people with mental retardation has stubbornly persisted and continues to infringe upon their civil rights."

Introduction

At the Alaska Bead Company, twenty-five-year-old Emily Ningeok carefully weighs out exactly two ounces of craft beads, places them in a small plastic bag, staples a tag on it, and puts the bag in the "done" pile. Working as quickly as she can, Ningeok fills fourteen bags in half an hour. She is an excellent part-time employee who works hard and gets along well with her coworkers. Ningeok is mentally handicapped, and therefore, despite her skills and pleasant personality, is lucky to be working at all. While employment discrimination based on race, ethnicity, and gender has diminished substantially in response to legislative and societal changes, prejudice against people with mental retardation has stubbornly persisted and continues to infringe upon their civil rights.

About 3 percent of Americans are affected by mental retardation—one family in ten will be touched by it in some way—according to the Association for Retarded Citizens (ARC). Retardation affects one hundred times as many people as total blindness. It is twelve times more common than cerebral palsy and thirty times more prevalent than neural tube defects such as spina bifida. Despite the prevalence of mental retardation in the general population, many people are uneasy with developmentally handicapped adults. Bob Russell, founder of Custom Manufacturing Services, a Kentucky company with a workforce of 175 mentally handicapped people, explains how employers' attitudes hurt both them and potential employees: "By looking constantly at people's intellectual limitations, [employers] are overlooking a lot of potential positives . . . [and] low expectations of mentally retarded people keeps them from reaching their potential."

Experts estimate that full-time employment rates for mentally handicapped adults range from 7 to 23 percent, with an even smaller percentage, 9 to 20 percent, employed part-time. Thus, most developmentally handicapped adults are either unemployed, work fewer hours per week than they would choose, or work at jobs below their skill level. According to ARC,

> The majority [of mentally handicapped adults] are either unemployed or underemployed, despite their desire, and willingness to engage in meaningful work in the community. Of those employed, many have had no choice but to

14

work in sheltered, segregated programs that separate people from their communities. Whatever the setting, few have had the opportunity to earn much money, acquire benefits, advance their careers, or plan for retirement.

While prejudice is not the only barrier to employment for mentally handicapped people—transportation difficulties and skill development are other problem areas—it is the most difficult one to overcome. Employers are often reluctant to recruit, hire, and train mentally handicapped individuals because they are not sure that they can accommodate the new hire's special needs, such as a more extensive training period or extended mentoring. R.H. Carter explains in the *Los Angeles Business Journal*, "While the accommodations for people with physical disabilities are largely mechanical and visible, the workplace adjustments for workers with mental . . . disabilities are mostly invisible. They consist primarily of policies, practices, attitudes, and language." Further, employers often worry that hiring a mentally handicapped person will create a safety risk, such as improper use of products or machinery, in the workplace. However, in a survey of employers in Oklahoma, 93 percent report that mentally handicapped employees present no greater risk than other employees. The President's Committee on Mental Retardation concurs, reporting safety records equivalent to employees without disabilities.

Moreover, 95 percent of the employers in the Oklahoma survey relate that hiring developmentally disabled people did not adversely affect employee health and benefit programs—another common reason cited for prejudice against mentally handicapped workers. Mentally handicapped workers were comparable to employees without disabilities in performance, attendance, and tenure. Jonah Kaufman, owner of thirteen McDonald's restaurants employing forty mentally handicapped adults says, "These people [mentally handicapped workers] never come in late and are rarely sick."

While the Civil Rights Act of 1964 and the Americans with Disabilities Act (ADA) of 1990 did a great deal to educate the public about the hireability of mentally handicapped citizens, the acts also raised concerns. Employers began to worry about being in compliance with the laws, concerned that their newly hired workers or the advocacy groups that represented them would sue them. The ADA opened doors to employment previously closed for some developmentally handicapped people, but it was not the cure for discrimination that the disabled community had hoped it would be. Other state and federal incentive programs—such as on-the-job-training reimbursements, the Job Training Partnership Act (JTPA), and the Targeted Jobs Tax Credit provision of the Internal Revenue Service—did entice some employers to hire mentally handicapped workers.

Despite all incentives, however, discrimination continues and mentally handicapped people do not fare well in the job market. Statistics that compare the employment rates for mentally and physically handicapped people provide a telling commentary on the American perception of people with mental retardation: Individuals with physical handicaps are less likely to be discriminated

15

against in employment than mentally handicapped people. ARC maintains that "while today's [mentally handicapped] youth appear to be doing better in the job market, they still are unemployed to a greater extent than youth with most other disabilities and those without disabilities." A survey of young mentally handicapped adults out of school three to five years revealed that 63 percent were not working.

Estimates place the cost in special services and lost wages as a result of unemployment or underemployment of developmentally handicapped people at about $6 billion a year. The toll in human suffering is incalculable—most people with mental retardation who are capable of working want to work. William Kiernan, director of the Institute for Community Inclusion in Boston, wrote in *Focus on Autism and Other Developmental Disabilities,*

> Employment is a means to economic independence, a route to social identification, and a source for personal networking for most adults in U.S. society. . . . Unfortunately, for many persons with mental retardation, employment and the associate benefits have not been a realistic option.

However, despite intense competition for even minimum-wage jobs, Kiernan is optimistic that employment discrimination against people with mental retardation will decrease in coming years. While tolerance for mentally handicapped people in the workplace has not kept pace with acceptance of physically handicapped workers, minorities, gays, and women, employers have learned the value of diversity and are beginning to understand the economic and social benefits it can bring to their businesses. Kiernan explains:

> The changing workforce, the increased emphasis on equality and opportunity, and the recognition that there is a need for a closer working relationship between employers and those charged with facilitating the entry into work of the nontraditional worker are all elements that in the coming years will create more jobs for persons with mental retardation.

Protecting the civil rights of all people within America's borders—citizen or not, handicapped or not, regardless of race, religion, or country of national origin—is one of the greatest responsibilities entrusted to America's leaders. The viewpoints in *Current Controversies: Civil Rights* debate many of the issues surrounding civil rights in the following chapters: Are Threats to Civil Rights a Serious Problem? Should Civil Rights Protections Be Increased? Is Affirmative Action Beneficial? Do Efforts to Prevent Terrorism Threaten Civil Rights? While all Americans treasure their civil rights, few can agree on how best to protect them.

Chapter 1

Are Threats to Civil Rights a Serious Problem?

Chapter Preface

"As blatant racism has diminished, 'sizism,' the prejudice against fat people, rears its ugly head as the most acceptable and marketable form of discrimination in the Western World," claims E.K. Daufin, an assistant professor at California State University at Los Angeles. Daufin is not alone in her assessment of discrimination against fat people. Susan C. Wooley, director of the eating disorders clinic at the University of Cincinnati, maintains that "we're running out of people we're allowed to hate, and to feel superior to. Fatness is the one thing left that seems to be a person's fault—which it isn't." The National Association to Advance Fat Acceptance (NAAFA), a non-profit organization committed to ending sizism, considers size discrimination a serious threat to the civil rights of millions of overweight Americans

Like racists and sexists, those who are prejudiced against fat people use myths and stereotypes to justify their discriminatory treatment of a specific group of people. Researchers have found that for many people, a fat person symbolizes loss of control, a reversion to infantile desires, failure, self-loathing, sloth, passivity, and gluttony. Esther Rothblum, a psychologist at the University of Vermont, explains that "the history of this country was influenced by the Puritans, and people are supposed to be in control, stoic, self-denying. When somebody looks hedonistic or self-indulgent, there's a tremendous animosity toward that person." Indeed, prejudice against fat people—especially heavy women—in the critical area of employment has cast them in the role of second-class citizens. They are seen as incompetent and undeserving of responsible, high-paying jobs. "In interview situations, employers bring their biases along with them," says NAAFA's Maryanne Bodolay. "They see us as lazy, not motivated, self-indulgent, and weak-willed. And they assume we're not good workers when really, we have to work harder and try harder than everybody else because of our appearance."

Statistics seem to support Bodolay's claim. According to a 2002 study in the journal *Health Economics*, obese women earned from 2.3 percent to 6.2 percent less than thinner women in the same profession; obese men earned from .7 percent to 2.6 percent less than their thinner counterparts. In her book *Tipping the Scales of Justice: Fighting Weight Based Discrimination*, Sondra Solovay notes that 16 percent of employers surveyed said that they would not hire obese women under any conditions.

However, obese people need not suffer the humiliation of employment discrimination without hope of redress. While the Civil Rights Act of 1964 does not specifically include overweight people in the list of protected classes, employers or prospective employers who apply size requirements in a discriminatory manner are considered to be in violation of the law and can be prosecuted. One state—Michigan—has a statute specifically outlawing size discrimination, and the District of Columbia prohibits discrimination based on "personal appearance."

To be sure, fat people often find their civil rights compromised when employers judge them by their weight rather than their abilities. Authors in the following chapter examine how other forms of prejudice threaten the civil rights of minority groups.

Racial Profiling Violates African Americans' and Hispanics' Civil Rights

by Malik Miah

About the author: *Malik Miah is an advisory editor for* Against the Current, *a magazine published by the Socialist organization Solidarity.*

It's happened to most Blacks at least once in our lifetime. Driving towards home or heading from work on the freeway a cop decides to pull you over for no reason. You wait in your car (you never get out first), hoping it's nothing. As you wait, the tension increases throughout your body. You keep your hands visible and crack no smile. Is it just a ticket? Or worse? (You wonder why African-Americans have high blood pressure.)

It's happened to me. In Detroit—my hometown—in 1970, for example, I was coming home in the late evening after attending Wayne State University.

I turned down my street on the northwest side of the city, and a cop car stopped me for no reason. I immediately became worried since back then Detroit cops were known for their extreme racism. Fortunately, they did nothing but check the car—and me—out. I was questioned like a common criminal, but I said nothing to provoke them. I knew better.

What I remember most about the incident was how relieved I felt after they left. Did I report it? Of course not. One thing you learn being a person of color, and a young male, is to "take" the everyday racism. You must pick your fights.

As American as Apple Pie

In fact, racial profiling is as American as apple pie. Before the civil rights movement ended legal segregation, governments, employers and cops knew they could humiliate and brutalize Blacks with impunity. Employers could deny African-Americans jobs and training without any fear of government or court action. Cops, who were mainly white and lived in the suburbs, could terrorize

Malik Miah, "The Reality of Racial Profiling," *Against the Current*, vol. 16, July/August 1999, pp. 5–6.

Blacks, especially young males, on the streets, in the parks, anytime they felt like it.

It is why most African-Americans see cops as a not-so-friendly force in our communities. (And that includes the African-American cops too.) The gap between white and Black perceptions of cops is based on real hard evidence—of being treated as second-class citizens, or worse.

Driving While Black (DWB) exposes the true underbelly of how the system still works. Middle-class Blacks and Latinos found out they are not exempt. They are also targets. It's not just for the poor guy driving a Ford pickup. Just as happened during the civil rights movement, middle-class Blacks are angry. They're not only filing lawsuits but they're joining protests against cop racism. And these protests—not the fact that the issue is "new"—is why the news media and the Clinton administration, as well as state and city governments, are taking up the issue.

According to the ACLU, [American Civil Liberties Union] more than a dozen states have legislation pending to begin collecting data on racial profiling. On June 9 [1999, then-President Bill] Clinton issued an executive order requiring the federal law enforcement agencies to collect demographic data on how they do their job.

Lobbying and lawsuits to gain legislation and to stop racial profiling has gotten little positive result until recently. What changed is the impact of mass protests demanding police accountability. The most significant protests have occurred in New York City in [1999].

Demonstrating Against Police Brutality

Demonstrations demanding justice after the murder of an unarmed West African immigrant, Amadou Diallo, sparked national interest. Diallo was shot at forty-one times by four New York City cops who claimed he posed a threat even though he had no weapon. Protests by civil rights and civil liberties groups at police headquarters took place daily to force action against the cops.

The public outrage over the Diallo case was fueled in part by the anger generated [in 1998] in a police brutality case involving the beating and torture of Abner Louima, a Black Haitian immigrant, in a Brooklyn police station. Louima survived the beating and was able to tell his story. The

"The cops use racial profiling to victimize, not to protect, our communities."

spotlight finally led a federal jury in New York to convict one cop involved in the beating after another pleaded guilty.

What these two cases exposed was something that every African-American (and Brown) person—particularly men—know quite well: The cops use racial profiling to victimize, not to protect, our communities. Civil rights and civil liberties groups demand the data to show how the statistics prove racism. In California, for example, the first decision made by the former Republican Governor [Pete] Wilson (and still followed by the new Democratic Governor [Gray] Davis) after affirmative action programs were ended in the state was to stop all collection of data by race—the only way to prove *de facto* segregation of minorities and bias for whites in all state jobs, contracts and educational opportunities.

> *"Being stopped by the police for no apparent reason is something that African-American and Hispanic motorists have lived with for decades."*

Is it a surprise that more Black men are in prison than college? Is it a surprise that the average white sees Blacks as prone to crime? The practice of the police and governments enforce the idea that people of color are really prone to crime and are not trustworthy.

Diallo's crime? He came out of his apartment to see why the cops were barging *into* his building. To the four cops, he was simply a Black male, and therefore a probable criminal; so shoot first to kill.

Louima was brutalized for no other reason than he is a Black man and an immigrant. The cops even joked about it as they terrorized him. How many other times did this happen but the victim died?

Institutionalized Racism

It's not just the New York City cops, or the FBI or state troopers who brutalize. Custom Service agents routinely single out people of color for questioning and humiliation. Have a Muslim name or look Arabic, expect close examination. They even admit they profile people, focusing on certain types who just "happen to be," in their majority, people of color. Who else could be drug runners and terrorists?

The New Jersey Turnpike state cops regularly stop Blacks and Latinos for no reason other than the color of their skin. Amazingly, they admitted using racial profiling to make these illegal stops. I guess they thought Blacks in Jersey would see them as more progressive than their New York neighbors who still deny using racial profiling for their busts.

In an excellent cover story in the June [1999] issue of the Black monthly magazine, *Emerge*, on DWB, the reporter Marcia Davis documents how extensive and pervasive racial profiling is across the country. Relying on personal horror stories and information provided by the ACLU, which has led the drive to end this form of racism, Davis notes: "Being stopped by the police for no apparent reason is something that African-American and Hispanic motorists have lived with for decades. Now it seems, at least, that in some quarters of the country, those complaints are being taken seriously. The challenge will be to find real solutions, not only for the problem of DWBs, but other chronic biases in policing and the entire criminal justice system."

Racism as a Tool of Control

This, of course, touches the root of the problem: the criminal justice system. The system is not primarily here to protect us or rehabilitate those who commit social crimes. Its purpose is to strike fear into the population in order to maintain control. Racism is an essential weapon in the control process. Racist justice (the use of the death penalty and disproportionate sentencing for Blacks for various drug violations) is to convince whites of all social strata that Blacks and other minorities are inclined to do crime. Thus we must be treated unfairly for the good of the majority. When most whites hear the words racial profiling and DWB, they believe it may be overdone but there is a valid reason for it.

The criminal justice system (an important tool for the capitalist system itself) is, of course, class based too. This is to convince the middle class to support limits on democratic rights to keep the poor in their place. Most middle-class Blacks accept this role of police agencies. They fear working-class and poor Blacks as much as their middle-class white neighbors.

Racism, however, doesn't recognize class divisions in the African-American population. Racist cops see skin color, not income, when they stop an African-American in a Mercedes. Even cops who are Black or Brown, but out of uniform, encounter this racism.

"Ninety percent of the people that they stop and infringe upon their rights get stopped and get humiliated," says police Major Aaron Campbell Jr., a cop in Dade County, Florida, for nearly thirty years. While driving to a house he was building in North Florida, he was pulled over early one evening in 1997:

"The incident, caught on videotape and now part of Campbell's own efforts to expose what he calls a 'racist game of smoke and mirrors,' ended in a scuffle with Orange County deputies. Campbell was peppered sprayed and arrested." [Source: ACLU.]

> *"When most whites hear the words racial profiling and DWB [Driving While Black], they believe it may be overdone but there is a valid reason for it."*

In North Carolina in 1998, Nelson Walker, a young Liberian attending college in North Carolina, was driving along I–95 in Maryland when he was pulled over by state police who said he wasn't wearing a seat belt. The officers detained him and his two passengers for two hours as they searched the car for illegal drugs, weapons, or other contraband.

Finding nothing, they proceeded to dismantle the car, removing part of a door panel, a seat panel and part of the sunroof. Finding nothing, the officers handed Walker a screwdriver, saying, "'You're going to need this' as they left the scene." (June 11, 1998, *The News & Observer,* Raleigh, North Carolina. Source: ACLU.)

Johnny Gammage wasn't so "lucky." While driving his cousin's Jaguar in Brentwood—a suburb of Pittsburgh—on October 12, 1995, he was pulled over.

⸱ cops said Gammage had run three red lights. One ordered Gammage out the car and said he reached [for] "a weapon."

It turned out to be a cell phone. The cops knocked it out of his hand, then proceeded to beat him with a flashlight, a collapsible baton and a blackjack. Gammage, who was unarmed, died handcuffed and ankle bound. (January 15, 1996, *People's* magazine. Source: ACLU.)

[Although a corner's jury recommended that all five face first-degree murder charges, one was acquitted of involuntary manslaughter by an all-white jury and a mistrial was declared against two others. (see *ATC* [*Against the Current*] 66, "Police Brutality and A Hot Autumn.")—ed.]

Laura Murphy, director of the Washington office of the ACLU said after Clinton issued the executive order, "This is just a mandate to gather statistics, not a mandate to solve the problem. But I don't want to be too negative. This is an important first step."

What will be decisive in the long run is using mass action to force whoever is president, governor or mayor to act. The daily protests in New York City kept the heat on the mayor and police chief to take some modest actions to rein in their cops.

Before the victory of the civil rights movements in the 1960s, many people thought old Jim Crow segregation could never be overturned without the overthrow of capitalism. Mass actions *did* end the old segregation and open the door to real changes in how people of color are treated. The rise of a Black middle class and better paid and skilled Black workforce is a direct result of those changes.

While causing radical change of the system is not yet possible, winning positive reform *can* be achieved. The use of discriminatory racial profiling can be pushed back by direct public pressure—as the New York City example shows.

Hate Crimes Against Arab Americans Are a Serious Problem

by Hussein Ibish

About the author: *Hussein Ibish is the communications director for the American Arab Anti-Discrimination Committee, an organization that works to protect civil rights and promote a balanced U.S. policy in the Middle East. He is a frequent spokesperson for the organization.*

The atrocities of September 11 [2001][1] provoked a backlash involving a surge of hate crimes against the Arab-American, Muslim, Sikh, South Asian and other communities perceived to be Middle Eastern. In September 2001, ADC [American-Arab Anti-Discrimination Committee] received an unprecedented number of reports from claimants in 41 states and the District of Columbia alleging violent incidents directed at Arab Americans or those perceived to be Arab Americans. ADC defines "violent incidents" as involving either physical violence of some kind or a direct threat of a specific act of violence.

In September 2001 alone, the number of personal attacks on Arabs and Arab Americans reported to ADC exceeded the number of such attacks cited in ADC's two year *1998–2000 Report on Hate Crimes and Discrimination against Arab Americans* (ADC 2001). In the first nine weeks following the September 11 [terrorist] attacks, ADC confirmed over 700 violent incidents directed at Arab Americans or those perceived to be Arab Americans. In the first nine months of 2002, by contrast, ADC had received 165 reports of violent incidents, 66% of reports received by the ADC legal department alleged physical and psychological attacks. Acts of vandalism and arson equaled 27% of claims; hate mail, threats and bomb threats 22%; beatings and physical attacks 16%; murders investigated as hate crimes 1%. Physical attacks include either battery

---

1. On September 11, 2001, the United States was attacked by Arab terrorists.

or destruction of property. Many of the cases of physical attacks included in this report occurred the week of September 11–18, 2001 (54% of battery reports, 67% of vandalism and arson reports, and five of the suspected or confirmed hate crime murders). As shown in the following case summaries, many of these incidents resulted in thousands of dollars worth of damage to mosques, businesses and homes. Others involved grievous bodily harm that resulted in hospitalization and maiming. ADC continues to receive cases of physical attacks, mostly reports of vandalism.

> *"Many of the cases of physical attacks . . . occurred the week of September 11–18, 2001."*

Local convictions include a death sentence in the case of Mark Anthony Stroman, a white supremacist who walked into a succession of convenience stores in the Dallas area, in the days after September 11 and killed a clerk from Pakistan and another from India, and partially blinded a third from Bangladesh. In addition to numerous successful local and state prosecutions, several federal criminal civil rights prosecutions have addressed acts of violence. In Salt Lake City, James Herrick was sentenced to 51 months incarceration on January 7, 2002, after pleading guilty to setting fire to a Pakistani restaurant in Salt Lake City on September 13, 2001. Patrick Cunningham of Seattle, Washington, pled guilty on May 9, 2002, to attempting to set fire to automobiles and shooting at worshipers at a mosque. Jason and Travis Kitts were charged with committing a federal hate crime in Knoxville, Tennessee. The Kitts brothers physically assaulted an Indian-American resident manager of a motel on September 24, 2001.

Meanwhile, federal charges are pending against several other defendants, alleging that the victims were targeted because of their perceived race, nationality, or religion. Among these are:

• Irving David Rubin, now deceased, and Earl Leslie Krugel, members of the Jewish Defense League, indicted in Los Angeles for conspiracy to bomb a mosque and the California office of United States Representative Darrell Issa.

• Charles D. Franklin indicted on April 17, 2002, for crashing a pick-up truck into a Tallahassee, Florida mosque.

Additionally, as this Report went to press, Robert Goldstein, the Florida podiatrist accused of plotting attacks on Islamic centers across the state was found competent to face criminal charges by a court-appointed psychiatrist. The competency finding clears the way for Goldstein to be indicted by a grand jury. He was arrested August 23, 2002, after Pinellas County sheriff's deputies found an arsenal of high-powered guns, Claymore mines and homemade bombs in his condominium when they responded to a domestic call. Agents subsequently found a typed, three-page "mission template" for a terrorist attack against Muslims in Florida.

Although psychological attacks, such as hate mail, threats and hate speech, occur more frequently than any other type of personal attack, these crimes often are left unreported. Legally, derogatory speech made against any individual or group constitutes a crime only if it directly incites physical violence, either in words or with non-verbal threats (such as a gun or throat-slitting motion with the fingers.) Otherwise, derogatory comments made against the national origin and/or religion of an individual are protected as free speech under the First Amendment of the Constitution. Threatening speech, on the other hand, may be prosecuted as a hate crime under most jurisdictions. In one of the most notable of these cases, Zachary J. Rolnik of Hanover, Massachusetts, pled guilty to making threatening telephone calls to James Zogby, President of the Arab American Institute (AAI). Rolnik pled guilty in federal district court on June 6, 2002, to interfering with Zogby's civil rights and was sentenced to two months in prison and assessed a $5,000 fine. He admitted placing a telephone call to Zogby in Washington on the morning of September 12, 2001, and leaving a voice mail message in which he threatened to kill him and his children. A similar case involving threats left in voice mail messages to ADC President Ziad Asali, M.D., is under DOJ [Department of Justice] civil rights investigation as this Report goes to press.

There have been guilty pleas in four other federal cases where threats were made to persons because of their perceived nationality:

• Thomas Iverson pled guilty to telephoning a bomb threat on September 29, 2001, against a Jordanian American liquor store in Beloit, Wisconsin. Iverson was sentenced to 27 months incarceration on April 12, 2002.

• Joe Luis Montez pled guilty to placing telephone calls on September 17, 2001, in Hewitt, Texas, threatening Sikhs employed at a truck stop. Montez was sentenced to 2 years probation and a $500 fine on January 30, 2002.

• Justin Scott-Priestly Bolen pled guilty on February 6, 2002, to interfering with the housing rights of a Pakistani-American family in Fenton, Michigan, by leaving a threatening message on their answering machine on October 10, 2001. Bolen was sentenced on May 14, 2002, to ten months incarceration.

• Wesley Fritts pled guilty in Madison, Wisconsin, to an anthrax hoax letter mailed to an Arab-American restaurant. Fritts was sentenced to 21 months incarceration on May 13, 2002.

Racial Discrimination in Mortgage Lending Is a Serious Problem

by the Urban Institute

About the author: *The Urban Institute is a national research center that provides independent analysis of government and private programs. The Institute prepared "What We Know About Mortgage Lending Discrimination," the report from which this viewpoint was excerpted, for the U.S. Department of Housing and Urban Development (HUD). The Institute's current research is focused on unmasking social problems that persist in prosperous times.*

A major element of the American dream is home of one's own in the neighborhood of one's choice. Owning a home is one of the primary ways of accumulating wealth in our society, a form of wealth acquisition that is especially protected in the U.S. tax code. Being a homeowner is also known to increase people's feelings of control over their lives and their sense of overall well-being. High rates of homeownership are believed to strengthen neighborhoods as well, by increasing residents' stake in the future of their communities.

But not all Americans enjoy equal access to the benefits of homeownership. Federal law prohibits discrimination in the home buying process, mandating that all would-be home buyers must be treated equally by real estate agents, lenders, appraisers, and insurance brokers. However, existing enforcement mechanisms may not be sufficient to guarantee equal treatment or equitable results. Indeed, research clearly shows that minorities still face substantial discrimination in the process of looking for a home to buy (or rent).

Many people believe that minorities also face discrimination when they try to obtain a mortgage—a necessity for most Americans wanting to buy a home. There is no question that minorities are less likely than whites to obtain mortgage financing and, if successful, receive less generous loan amounts and terms. But whether these differences are the result of discrimination—rather

Urban Institute, "What We Know About Mortgage Lending Discrimination," *Urban Institute Report*, September 15, 1999.

than the inevitable result of objectively lower creditworthiness—is still debated in some quarters. The problem here is not that analysts or practitioners have ignored the question of discrimination in mortgage lending. Many research and investigative studies have addressed certain facets of it, using different data sets and analytic techniques to study various outcomes. The problem is that these studies have not produced a clear consensus on a set of conclusions. . . .

Our review of the existing research evidence concludes that minority homebuyers in the United States do face discrimination from mortgage lending institutions. Discrimination in home mortgage lending takes two forms—differential treatment and disparate impact—and in many instances, it is difficult, if not impossible to disentangle the two. Although significant gaps remain in what we know, a substantial body of objective and credible statistical evidence strongly indicates that discrimination persists:

Finding #1

Discrimination can begin at the early stages of the mortgage lending process, including pre-application inquiries by would-be-borrowers. This analysis reviewed results from HUD [Department of Housing and Urban Development]-funded "paired testing" that was carried out in selected cities. Testers of different races, who were matched on credit history and other traits, approached lenders with the same types of mortgage needs. Overall, minorities were less likely to receive information about loan products, received less time and information from loan officers, and were quoted higher interest rates in most of the cities where tests were conducted.

Finding #2

At later stages of the process, racial disparities in loan denial rates cannot be "explained away" by differences in credit worthiness or by technical factors affecting the analyses. Statistical re-analysis of data assembled by the Federal Reserve Bank of Boston (data that include measures of creditworthiness and other important factors) finds large differences in loan denial rates between minority and white applicants, and these differences cannot be explained away by data or statistical problems asserted by prior critics of the "Boston Fed" study. This analysis presents substantial evidence that discrimination exists, shifting the "burden of proof" to those who would argue that these differences are entirely due to racially neutral underwriting criteria.

Finding #3

Good intentions—on the part of lenders—are not enough. In-depth examination of the mortgage loan origination process from an individual lender's perspective suggests that even among institutions with good intentions, and where loan officers take pride in working with borrowers who need more help on loan applications, minority customers may not be receiving equal treatment. The evidence on organizational change suggests that achieving significant reductions in lending discrimination may require such changes in business practices as: improving employee awareness of and attitudes toward fair lending obligations; making the "business case" for fair lending and its importance to the firm; implementing clear incentives that support change; monitoring employee performance on fair lending; tackling underwriting standards that have disproportionate, negative effects on minorities but serve no clear business purposes; and more. . . .

Different Forms of Discrimination

Discrimination in mortgage lending can take two different forms. It is important to understand the distinctions clearly, because the different forms of discrimination may require different measurement strategies, as well as different remedies. The fundamental distinction is between differential treatment and disparate impact discrimination.

Differential treatment discrimination occurs when equally qualified individuals are treated differently due to their race or ethnicity. In mortgage lending, differential treatment might mean that minority applicants are more likely than whites to be discouraged from applying for a loan, to have their loan application rejected, or to receive unfavorable loan terms—even after taking into account characteristics of the applicant, property, and loan request that affect creditworthiness. A finding of differential treatment discrimination means that minorities receive less favorable treatment from a given lender than majority applicants with the same credit-related characteristics (as observable by the lender).

Disparate impact discrimination occurs when a lending policy, which may appear to be color-blind in the way it treats mortgage loan applicants, disqualifies a larger share of minorities than whites, but cannot be justified as a business necessity. A widely cited example is the policy of minimum mortgage loan amounts—setting a dollar limit below which a lending institution will not issue mortgages. More minorities than whites will be adversely affected by any given loan cut-off, because—on average—minorities have lower incomes than whites and can only afford less costly houses. Policies such as minimum loan amounts, which disproportionately affect minorities, are illegal unless they serve an explicit business necessity. If these policies do not accurately reflect creditworthiness, or if they could be replaced by policies serving the same business purpose with less of a disproportionate effect on minorities, then they are deemed under Federal law to be discriminatory.

> *"Existing research evidence concludes that minority homebuyers in the United States do face discrimination from mortgage lending institutions."*

The point for public policy is that policies which are discriminatory in effect may have adverse consequences of much greater magnitude than practices that treat individuals differently on the basis of their race. Federal policy makes disparate impact discrimination illegal so that institutional policies do not simply perpetuate patterns of racial inequality, many of which are the consequence of past discrimination. In other words, achieving a world of truly fair lending will require remedies that go beyond color-blindness.

Possible Motives for Discrimination

The most straightforward explanation for why discrimination occurs is prejudice (often referred to by analysts as taste-based discrimination). If lenders—or their employees—are prejudiced against minorities, they consider them to be inherently inferior and prefer not to interact with them or have them as customers. The lending industry has long argued that it does not discriminate, because doing so would go against the very reason for being in business—maximizing profits. It is not the color of a customer's skin that matters, according to an often-quoted statement of this viewpoint, but the color of his or her money. This argument does not dispose of the discrimination issue, however. First, it is entirely possible for prejudice to persist among profit-motivated businesses, due to market imperfections, information barriers, and the large number of people who participate in a loan-approval decision. In fact, suggestive, though not definitive, evidence that prejudice may indeed be a factor at work comes from one study in which black-white disparities in loan approval rates decline as minority representation in either a lender's overall workforce or its management staff increases.

> *"Overall, minorities were less likely to receive information about loan products, received less time and information from loan officers, and were quoted higher interest rates."*

Moreover, even if there is no "taste-based" discrimination in the industry, discrimination may in fact be in a mortgage lender's perceived economic self-interest. Discrimination for this type of reason is referred to as economic discrimination, to distinguish it from discrimination due to prejudice. The key point here is that some factors that influence a lender's expected rate of return may also be highly correlated with race or ethnicity. For example, minorities may be less likely than whites to have affluent family members who can help them out if they get into a financial bind, or they may be more likely to be laid off in the event of an economic downturn. If lenders think that race is a reliable proxy for factors they cannot easily observe that affect credit risk, they will have an economic incentive to discriminate against minorities. Thus, denying mortgage credit to a minority applicant on the basis of information that is valid for minorities on average—but not necessarily for the individual in question—may be economically rational. But it is still discrimination, and it is illegal.

Recent attention has focused on cultural affinity as another possible reason for discrimination. This argument attributes discrimination to the lack of affinity among white loan officers for the culture of certain minority groups. Because they feel less comfortable with minority borrowers, or because they are not able to understand the way minorities communicate, loan officers may exert less effort to determine creditworthiness or to help minority borrowers meet underwriting criteria. The literature suggests several possible explanations for why this type of behavior might be occurring, but most turn out to be forms of either prejudice or economic discrimination. Another version of the cultural affinity argument is that blacks and whites tend to sort themselves by lender—black to black, white to white—and the resulting pattern of loan offerings is discriminatory to minorities. Indeed, there is some suggestive evidence that applicants may sort themselves by race in selecting lenders, but not that this form of "cultural affinity" results in differential loan denial rates.

Prohibiting Same-Sex Marriage Violates Gays' and Lesbians' Civil Rights

by the American Civil Liberties Union of Texas

About the author: *The American Civil Liberties Union (ACLU) is a national organization that fights to safeguard Americans' civil rights. The following viewpoint was written by the Texas chapter of the ACLU.*

Civil marriage is the primary institution in our society for recognizing our most intimate, committed relationships. It is also the device our society uses to identify our partners for a range of rights and responsibilities—everything from retirement programs to hospital visitations.

Until 1967, many states prohibited interracial marriages, claiming these unions were a deviation from the "natural order." In that year, the Supreme Court struck down these bans, decreeing they deprived people of their "fundamental right to marry." Currently, lesbian and gay men across the country are fighting for the freedom to marry in order to secure this same right. Spurred by a court case in Hawai'i, the battle has recently moved to center stage and become one of the burning issues of our time.

The Hawai'i Case

In December of 1996, a trial court in Hawai'i ruled that the state's ban on same-sex marriage violates the equal protection clause of the Hawai'i constitution. The ruling—the first of its kind in the nation's history—held that Hawai'i had failed to meet its burden to offer a "compelling" reason to maintain a discriminatory practice. Earlier the Hawai'i Supreme Court had held the state's refusal to honor same-sex marriages violates the Hawai'i constitution's ban on sex discrimination, just as bans on interracial marriages violated anti-discrimination laws. The trial court ruling was appealed to the state Supreme Court, which unfortunately, rendered a decision against the plaintiffs' protest of the ban to marry. Because the case involved the state, and not federal, constitutional issues, the Hawai'i Supreme Court has the final word on this particular case.

Had this litigation been successful in compelling the state to allow lesbian and gay couples to marry, another issue would have had to been addressed: other states would have had to decide how to treat those legally married couples if they move to or visit another state, or if couples travel to Hawai'i to marry. However, while this case was pending, some state legislatures decided to address these concerns before the decision was rendered. In the past few years, bills banning same-sex marriage have been introduced in 38 states. Although 22 states rejected these proposals, 16 states passed the bills. Two

> *"Marriage is a basic human right which cannot be denied to anybody."*

governors have signed executive orders preventing same-sex marriages. In addition, the federal government has stepped in and passed the "Defense of Marriage Act," designed to ban federal recognition of same-sex marriages and allow state governments to ignore same-sex marriages performed in different states.

Lesbian and gay couples are currently denied the right to marry in all 50 states. However, as the Supreme Court ruled in *Zablocki v. Redhail* (1978), marriage is a basic human right which cannot be denied anybody. If a lesbian or gay couple want to marry and commit themselves to each other, why should anyone interfere? Marriage is a personal decision that belongs to the two consenting adults in the relationship, not the government.

Marriage is also a device our society uses to identify our partners for an enormous range of practical situations. Because they are denied their basic right to marry, gay and lesbian couples are prohibited from enjoying the fundamental privileges and responsibilities the majority of people take for granted. Some of the many rights denied gay and lesbian couples include the right to:
- visit a partner or a partner's child in a hospital
- inherit from a partner if she or he doesn't leave a valid will
- obtain joint health, home and auto insurance policies
- enter joint rental agreements
- make medical decisions on a partner's behalf
- take bereavement or sick leave to care for a partner or a partner's child
- choose a final resting place for a deceased partner
- get an equitable division of property in a divorce
- obtain wrongful death benefits for a surviving partner and child
- have the right to determine child custody, visitation and child support issues in a divorce
- have joint adoptive or foster care parenting rights
- have a spouse covered under Medicare and Social Security
- file joint tax returns

- obtain veterans' discounts on medical care, education and home loans
- sponsor spouse in applying for residency status for partners from foreign nations

Marriage Is a Basic Human Right

The ACLU supports legal recognition of lesbian and gay relationships, including the right to marry. Such recognition is imperative for the complete legal equality of lesbian and gay individuals. The ACLU has also endorsed the "marriage resolution" developed by a coalition of groups working for the right of lesbian and gay people to marry. It states:

> Because marriage is a basic human right and an individual personal choice, RESOLVED, the State should not interfere with same-gender couples who choose to marry and share fully and equally in the rights, responsibilities, and commitment of civil marriage.

> "Marriage is a basic human right. You cannot tell people they cannot fall in love. Dr. Martin Luther King, Jr. used to say when people talked about interracial marriage and I quote, 'races do not fall in love and get married. Individuals fall in love and get married.'"

> *Testimony of Rep. John Lewis of Georgia before*
> *Congress on the Defense of Marriage Act, 7/1/96*

> "It will be up to each church to determine whether or not to conduct these marriages. This is a very different question than whether or not there are civil or State sponsored same-gender marriages. Regardless of the outcome of the court case, no church or clergy will be forced . . . to recognize same-gender marriages."

> *Clergy Coalition for Equality and Diversity,*
> *Christian and Same-Gender Marriage, 8/96*

Marriage is not premised on procreation. (1965 U.S. Supreme Court ruling in *Griswold v. Connecticut.*) Besides, many married couples do not and cannot have children while many lesbian and gay couples do have and raise children.

The Problem of Racial Profiling Is Exaggerated

by Dinesh D'Souza

About the author: *Dinesh D'Souza is a media fellow at the Hoover Institution and a John M. Olin Scholar at the American Enterprise Institute. The Hoover Institution and the American Enterprise Institute are conservative think tanks devoted to social research.*

Two Los Angeles police officers were cruising the city's highways when they saw a black man who looked as if he might be a drug dealer. So they pulled over his car, only to discover that their suspect was Christopher Darden, coprosecutor in the O.J. Simpson trial.

The cops cheerfully waved Darden on, but he was not amused. Speaking at a recent forum in San Francisco, Darden said he found such incidents "demeaning" and "humiliating," and he accused the police of routinely stopping black men in the belief that they are potential criminals. "Just about everyone I know has been stopped—ministers, doctors, lawyers, professional athletes," he said.

Law enforcement officers call "profiling" likely criminals a necessary part of police work, but African Americans call the practice of being pulled over simply because of the color of their skin "driving while black." Cops aren't the only offending group. Many blacks accuse big-city cabdrivers of refusing to pick up young black males, especially at night. African American men also complain that storekeepers follow them around, as if to prevent stealing, and that women who pass them on the street clutch their purses.

Racial Profiling May Not Be Racism

The American Civil Liberties Union recently released a report that cited mounting evidence of racially motivated police stops. Some members of Congress and state legislators are demanding that the practice be outlawed. Cabdrivers are being fined and even losing their licenses for passing up young black males. Civil rights leaders are calling for much tougher measures to stop what one terms "a shameful resurgence of racism." Yet in these cases, it is not clear that racism is involved. In Washington, D.C., for example, few of the cabdrivers accused of bigotry for passing up young black males are white. Many are immigrants from El Salvador, Nigeria, Pakistan, and the West Indies, and African American cabdrivers apparently act similarly.

At this point, sociologists are prone to launch into tortuous speculations about how historically victimized groups "internalize" their white oppressors' bigotry. But the explanation for the actions of the nonwhite cabdriver can far more simply and plausibly be attributed to two key facts. First, black males are six to ten times more likely to be convicted of violent crimes than

> *"Although rational discrimination against African Americans is a social problem, its magnitude should not be exaggerated."*

white males. Second, more than 25 percent of black males between the ages of fifteen and thirty-five are, at any given time, in prison, on probation, or on parole. (For whites, the comparable figure is about 5 percent.) Far from being a myth, the reality is that young black males are, by far, the most violent group in U.S. society.

These are uncomfortable social facts, but they are facts. Consequently, the treatment accorded young African American males by police officers, cabdrivers, storekeepers, and others cannot be attributed to irrational prejudice. It is more likely the product of rational discrimination. In a situation in which we have limited information about individuals (cabdrivers, for instance, are not in a position to know their clients personally), we must make group judgments based on probability.

Rational Discrimination Makes Sense

The concept of rational discrimination is easier to grasp if we look outside the racial context. Insurance companies, for example, charge teenage boys higher car insurance rates than teenage girls (or older drivers, for that matter). The reason isn't sexism or antimale prejudice; the statistical reality is that, on average, teenage boys are far more likely than teenage girls to bash their cars. So the insurance company is treating groups differently because they behave differently.

Although rational discrimination against African Americans is a social problem, its magnitude should not be exaggerated. Strictly speaking, it makes no sense for a bank manager to refuse to hire a black teller because blacks as a group have a high crime rate; the manager can easily investigate whether this particular African American job seeker has a criminal record. So also mortgage lenders cannot rationally refuse loans to blacks on the grounds that blacks pose a higher repayment risk; again, the lender can look at each applicant's income and credit history.

Still, rational discrimination is a fact of everyday life, and what to do about it poses a genuine public policy problem. Just because discrimination can be rational does not mean it is always moral. Indeed, the rational discrimination of cops, cabdrivers, and storekeepers is very unfair to the law-abiding African American who has done nothing wrong but is treated as a potential criminal. Yet before we approve harsh punishments against those who practice rational discrimination, we should recall that their only offense is using common sense. Shouldn't African Americans who are legitimately outraged at being victimized by discrimination direct their anger not at cabdrivers or police officers but at the black thieves, muggers, and crack dealers who are giving the entire group a bad name?

The Difference Between Public and Private Is Clear

My solution is that all forms of racial discrimination, including rational discrimination, should be illegal in the public sector. This means that police officers, who are agents of the state, should not be permitted to use race in deciding whether to question potential muggers or stop suspected drug dealers. The reason: We have a constitutional right to be treated equally under the law, meaning the government has no right to discriminate on the basis of race or color.

This point of principle will seem naive to those who ask about its cost in terms of police efficiency. The prudent answer is that there are other (in my view, more important) costs to be weighed. Government-sponsored rational discrimination has the cataclysmic social effect of polarizing African Americans who play by the rules and still cannot avoid being discriminated against. Even law-abiding blacks become enemies of the system because they find themselves treated that way.

In the private sector, we should be more flexible in dealing with rational discrimination. I think the campaign to go after cabdrivers for alleged bigotry is especially foolish. Of course, as a "person of color" myself, I'd be annoyed and indignant if I could not get a taxi. Yet my right to get a cab, which is the right not to be inconvenienced, seems less important than the cabdriver's right to protect his life and property. In cases such as this, it is better for the government to do nothing.

The Incidence of Hate Crimes Directed Against Arab Americans Is Exaggerated

by Michelle Malkin

About the author: *Michelle Malkin is a nationally syndicated columnist and the author of* Invasion: How America Still Welcomes Terrorists, Criminals, and Other Foreign Menaces to Our Shores.

Mazhar Tabesh, Nezar "Mike" Maad, and Aqil Yassom Al-Timimi all have something in common. They were held up by Muslim activists as innocent victims of the "post-September 11 [2001, terrorist attacks] backlash." They milked the compassion of their communities. They won sympathy from the media and politicians.

And now it appears they were all hate crime hucksters who cried 'racism' to cash in on the terrorist attacks.

Mazhar Tabesh, a naturalized American originally from Pakistan, co-owned a motel in Heber City, Utah. Last July, someone set the lodge ablaze, causing nearly $100,000 in damage.

"We are really scared because we are Muslim—probably the only Muslims in the area—and we are the target," Tabesh declared. "It's scary." Tabesh complained of receiving threatening calls from anonymous hatemongers who "told us they would get us if we didn't get out."

Utah residents organized a benefit concert and raised $1,400 for Tabesh's family. The national press jumped on the bandwagon: "Immigrant Family Feels Post-9/11 Rage," blared a *Los Angeles Times* headline. The accompanying story suggested that "white supremacists and skinheads living in the area" might be to blame.

But the chief suspect turned out to be Mazhar Tabesh himself. Prosecutors say Tabesh invented a "mystery man" arsonist and lied about witnessing the non-existent lodger running from the hotel after the fire started. His motive? A Heber City police officer testified at a preliminary hearing that Tabesh was losing about $5,900 a month on the motel and still owed $450,000 on the mortgage.

Tabesh will stand trial . . . on first-degree felony aggravated arson charges. Don't count on the *Los Angeles Times* to cover it.

Alleged Hate Crimes Turn Out to Be Hoaxes

The tale of Nezar "Mike" Maad follows the same basic plot. Maad, an Arab-American businessman and "tolerance advocate," owned a print shop in Anchorage, Alaska. On Sept. 21, 2001, someone destroyed equipment and spray-painted "We hate Arabs" inside the store. Community leaders created the "Not in Our Town" fund, a city-backed charity which raised a whopping $75,000 for Maad. A local newspaper editorial declared unequivocally that the incident "was a hate crime. It was vandalism. It was a statement against bedrock American values . . ."

Five months after Maad was "victimized," a jury convicted him of federal fraud charges. During the hate crime investigation, agents discovered that Maad had lied on bank loan applications and federal forms about his business finances and prior criminal convictions. Nevertheless, Maad received a reduced sentence of six months' prison time.

> *"They were all hate crime hucksters who cried 'racism' to cash in on the terrorist attacks."*

The FBI dropped its hate crime investigation; Maad and his wife remain the prime suspects in the languishing property damage case.

In Nashville, Tenn., Iraqi-American Aqil Yassom Al-Timmi claimed someone set his Chevy truck on fire after the Sept. 11 attacks because he was of Arab descent. Although local TV stations ate up the hate crime angle, one keen reporter remained skeptical and raised the strong possibility of an insurance fraud scheme. Writing in the *Nashville Scene*, Matt Pulle reported that no notes or graffiti were left at the crime scene. Emergency personnel were immediately suspicious of Al-Timimi, who reportedly pressed them to alert the media as soon as they arrived at Al-Timimi's home.

Sources said they suspected Al-Timmi was the perpetrator all along, but more than a year and a half after the fire, the case has languished. Al-Timmi, the supposed victim of hateful wrongdoing, hasn't been heard from since. "If he was playing us," Pulle told me, "he did a perfect job."

The FBI and Justice Department have vociferously condemned and aggressively prosecuted a string of anthrax hoaxes that followed the September 11 attacks. But when it comes to cracking down on hate crime hoaxes by Arabs and Muslims, the feds—too busy conducting politically correct "outreach" with

Muslim leaders who pooh-pooh hate crime fraud—have been appallingly negligent. There is no way of knowing whether fake hate crimes outnumber real anti-Muslim crimes because no law enforcement agency keeps track. (Note to frustrated cops: Send me your suspected hoax cases and let's get started.)

Hoax crimes waste precious investigative resources, exacerbate racial tension, create terror, and corrode goodwill. It's a shame so many in the media are more concerned with protecting the twisted cult of victimhood than with exposing hard truths.

Racial Discrimination Is Uncommon in Mortgage Lending

by George J. Benston

About the author: *George J. Benston is the John H. Harland Professor of Finance, Accounting, and Economics of the Goizueta Business School at Emory University, and a member of the Shadow Financial Regulatory Committee, a private group of academic economists and lawyers who specialize in financial services.*

Congressional attempts to enact banking and financial services reform in recent years have stumbled over the Community Reinvestment Act. That act originally was meant to deal with "redlining," the alleged refusal of banks to lend to residents of poorer urban, often racial-minority areas. But critics maintain that qualified applicants do not, in fact, suffer unwarranted discrimination and that CRA simply adds to the costs of banking, in the end often harming the very consumers the act was meant to protect.

CRA, enacted in 1977, and its 1975 predecessor, the Home Mortgage Disclosure Act, were initially intended simply to collect data on where banks lend money. However, over the years HMDA and CRA reporting costs have increased. Further, CRA is used to delay or prevent banks' acquiring or merging with other banks, closing branches, and the like when no illegal acts are involved.

HMDA and CRA have yielded few benefits to consumers. Researchers using the best available data find very little discernible home-mortgage lending discrimination based on area, race, sex, or ethnic origin. Furthermore, interstate banking; wider branching; and improved technology, which has engendered nationwide—indeed, global—competition, have meant greater availability or mortgage loans. Today there is no indication that qualified borrowers are turned down. . . .

No Evidence of Redlining Was Found

Academic researchers have studied the redlining allegation and found it wanting. Those studies did not rely on HMDA data alone, because those data did not provide information on mortgage terms, borrowers financial situations and credit histories, the supply of mortgages from lenders other than banks and thrifts, and, of great importance, the demand for mortgages in central-city compared with suburban areas. Indeed, many studies did not use the HMDA data at all.

Two such studies compared the demand for and supply of home mortgages in four cities—Rochester, New York; Cincinnati, Ohio; Indianapolis, Indiana; and Nashville, Tennessee. My colleagues and I chose those cities because community groups claimed that their central areas were redlined. We gathered data on mortgages made in the allegedly redlined central areas and roughly comparable suburbs of those cities; our data included interest rates, maturities, and down payments, as well as house prices and characteristics of properties. We included loans made by mortgage bankers and other lenders. Buyers of homes in the older, central-city neighborhoods and buyers of homes in suburban areas of the same cities were interviewed to learn of their mortgage-related problems. Neither group experienced much difficulty in obtaining the mortgages (FHA [Federal Housing Authority] or conventional) they wanted. In particular, buyers of suburban homes said they were not kept from buying homes in the central cities because of problems in obtaining mortgages. We estimated unmet demand for mortgages by interviewing central-city homeowners who had tried to sell their houses. Those people, we reasoned, would know whether or not potential buyers had problems getting mortgages, perhaps because of redlining. Almost none said that a sale had not been made for that reason (and those few who complained said that only blacks could get loans). Nor did homeowners in the central cities complain that they were unable to obtain home improvement loans. Other well-structured studies also found no evidence of redlining or unwarranted geographic discrimination.

> *"Researchers using the best available data find very little discernible home-mortgage lending discrimination based on area, race, sex, or ethnic origin."*

Thus, the claim that lenders redlined or were biased in making loans for the purchase of homes in central cities is not supported. Nor did the studies find that financial institutions discriminated against actual or potential borrowers on the basis of the racial or ethnic composition of neighborhoods.

Newspapers Allege Racial Discrimination

Renewed concerns that loans were being denied to potential homeowners, in this instance on the basis of race, were themselves based on several factors. A number of newspapers published exposés beginning in 1988 that analyzed the

HMDA data that were readily available from the Federal Reserve Board in computer-readable form. The *Atlanta Journal-Constitution* published a series in May 1988 that was awarded a Pulitzer Prize. A *Detroit Free Press* series ran in June 1988, and the *Washington Post* series was published in June 1993. Those articles included maps and charts showing the racial composition of census tracts together with the number of mortgages made by reporting banks and thrifts [savings and loan associations and credit unions]. Those data, which still did not include loans made by mortgage bankers and privately funded mortgages, gave the impression that banks and thrifts were making fewer loans than were demanded in predominantly black areas.

In 1989 HMDA was amended as part of the Financial Institutions Reform, Recovery, and Enforcement Act. That amendment required all mortgage lenders, not just banks and thrifts but mortgage banks as well, to report the race or ethnic origin, gender, and annual gross income of loan applicants. A Federal Reserve Board analysis of those 1990 data, covered widely in the press, revealed that African-Americans were more likely than other racial groups to use Federal Housing Authority or Veterans Administration loans, 52 percent compared to 25 percent of white borrowers. Further, two-thirds of lower-income black homebuyers purchased homes in the inner city, compared to two-fifths of whites. In addition, acceptances of loan applications were considerably lower in largely minority census tracts, 57 percent compared to 76 percent. Press reports especially focused on figures that seemed to show higher rates of denials of African-American and Hispanic applicants who had about the same reported income as whites. Federal Reserve Board economists tried to explain that the HMDA data did not take account of differences in the mortgage applicants' wealth as well as liabilities, employment history, and credit record, among other relevant variables that lenders should and do consider. But reporters downplayed or ignored those points.

In 1992 researchers at the Federal Reserve Bank of Boston attempted to deal with the limitations of the HMDA data by collecting information on some 30 variables that they believed were related to lending decisions. They found that much, but not all, of the difference between minority and non-minority denial rates was explained by those variables. Their finding of an average remaining black denial rate of 17 percent compared to a denial rate of 11 percent for whites was widely publicized.

"There is very little evidence of racial discrimination by any banks or thrifts [savings and loan associations and credit unions]."

Subsequently, David Horne, an economist at the Federal Deposit Insurance Corporation, analyzed the 70 FDIC-supervised banks studied by the Boston Fed. As reported in his 1997 study, Horne found some important mistakes in the data. For example, 69 applicants were recorded as having negative net worth (57 of them were approved for mortgages), and 116 applications were for loans that were supposed to have been excluded from the study (e.g., refinancings and investments). He found that including more relevant measures of the borrowers' credit history, such as past delinquencies and whether the borrower met the lenders' credit standards, the lenders' inability to verify the data submitted by the applicant, and information about the borrowers' ability to cover closing costs, explained the divergence in denial rates of black and white applicants. Furthermore, 49 of the 70 banks (70 percent) did not reject any minority loan applications; 2 of the remaining 21 banks were responsible for over half the denials of black applicants. Both of those banks, one of which was minority owned, had conducted extensive minority outreach programs and participated actively in affordable-housing programs. In addition, Harold Black applied the Boston Fed model to black- and white-owned banks operating in the same standard metropolitan statistical area. He found that black applicants were denied loans at significantly higher rates by the black-owned than by the white-owned banks.

It is neither surprising nor evidence of racial discrimination that banks specializing in loans to minorities have high denial rates. Those banks are likely to get a large number of marginal applicants and, hence, will have a relatively large percentage of denials. On the other hand, a bank that discriminated against African-Americans would have had a very low denial rate for those borrowers, if that bank let realtors know that it would consider applications only from financially "very well qualified" individuals and that it would "very carefully" scrutinize applications by "certain" individuals.

Defaults by Black Mortgagors

Data on defaults might seem to be a good way of learning whether lenders discriminate against African-Americans. If lenders discriminated by accepting only the most credit-worthy black applicants while accepting marginally qualified white applicants, whites would default proportionately more than blacks. In fact, there are no studies that report this finding, and several that report the contrary.

However, the fact that the available data show higher average default rates for black than for white mortgagors should not be interpreted as demonstrating that lenders discriminate against whites, that is, accept only the best-qualified white borrowers but marginally qualified black borrowers. Higher default rates for blacks compared to whites need not be racially determined any more than a higher rate of denial is racially determined. Rather, both statistics could be due to other factors that happen to be associated with the borrowers' race.

A 1996 analysis by Robert Avery and colleagues examined factors related to defaults on mortgages made through special "affordable-housing" programs to low- and moderate-income households. That inquiry found that the Federal Home Loan Mortgage Corporation's (Freddie Mac's) "Affordable Gold" loans, which go to poorer applicants, had a 60-day delinquency rate that was about 50 percent higher than that of a control group of traditionally underwritten mortgages with similar loan-to-value ratios and dates of origination for similar types of property in similar regions of the country. The most important reason for the higher delinquencies was a shortfall of mortgagors' funds to make down payments and other outlays. Indeed, Affordable Gold mortgagors who were allowed to meet part of the minimum down-payment requirement with funds provided by a third party had delinquency rates four times higher than the control group. In those cases loans were made to individuals with marginal qualifications, exemplified by the fact that they could not meet down payment requirements. The mortgagors' race was not the relevant factor.

Three private mortgage insurance companies, Mortgage Guarantee Insurance Corporation, GE Capital Mortgage Insurance Corporation, and United Guarantee Corp., also analyzed delinquencies among their "affordable-housing" mortgagors. They also found much higher delinquency rates on loans for which the borrower received much of the down payment from the seller or another third party. Further, they found much higher delinquency rates among mortgagors with no or adverse credit histories, higher ratios of debt payments to income than the traditional guideline levels, and less than one or two months of cash reserves at closing.

Recall that, to reanalyze the Boston Fed's data, FDIC researcher David Horne used measures of credit risk similar to those found to be related to defaults. With those variables included, there was no evidence of racial discrimination. Thus, it appears that there is reason to doubt that Boston banks denied mortgages to African-Americans because of their race. Indeed, there is very little evidence of racial discrimination by any banks or thrifts.

Prohibiting Same-Sex Marriage Is Not a Violation of Civil Rights

by David Orland

About the author: *David Orland is a columnist for* Boundless, *the webzine of Focus on the Family, a conservative Christian organization.*

If you've ever tried to discuss gay unions with someone who supports them, you know how difficult this can be. One is instantly branded a homophobe, a Christian reactionary, a right wing yokel and there the conversation ends, at least as far as your interlocutor is concerned. Unfortunately, such conversations perfectly mirror the national conversation about same-sex unions; they are one-sided and deaf.

My first run-in with the emerging orthodoxy regarding gay unions—often referred to by its euphemism, "domestic partnership"—occurred about two years ago [in 1998]. Reading the papers over a pot of coffee one Sunday afternoon with my then girlfriend, I came across an editorial on the subject. At this time, the "gay community" had just begun in earnest its efforts to force state legislatures to confer a legal status on homosexual unions and the editorial, which came out in support of these efforts, was overheated and impassioned in the way such editorials nearly always are. I guess I chuckled to myself because my girlfriend asked what it was. "Oh nothing," I remember replying with a smile and heavy irony, "just another article about why the cause of gay "marriage" is so moral and important."

Her smile disappeared. I suspected—indeed, I knew, somewhere in my belly—that I had made a serious mistake. "And what's so funny about that," she asked, her voice lowering in a sinister and unprecedented way. "Oh, nothing much," I answered, trying to avert disaster, "it's not so funny but it is kind of funny, you must admit." But she persisted: "why is it kind of funny?" Something told me I had been here before, which is probably why, rather than dropping the issue, I decided to defend myself. At first, I tried in a more or less incoherent way to point out what I considered the inherent silliness of the editorial's moral posturing. But with each attempt to sidestep a truly nasty argument, my girlfriend's indignation grew. Before very long (as is the way with such discussions), I had been resolutely labeled a "homophobe", an epithet which—with the help of its pseudo-scientific Latin suffix—conveniently renders pathological all deviations from the orthodox. "I know what you're going to say," she concluded triumphantly, smirking like a champion of dorm room contention, "you're going to say that homosexuality is immoral!"

> *"To justify giving privileges ... to some particular group in society, the benefit of doing so for society at large must first be shown."*

In fact, that wasn't what I was going to say. I knew that the argument that same-sex unions are sexually immoral would be the last thing to convince my agnostic girlfriend. Besides, a much different kind of argument had occurred to me. What, I asked, did the supporters of domestic partnership hope to gain? Legal recognition on par with heterosexual marriage, she answered. And what did such recognition entail, aside from some more or less vague sense of legitimacy? A series of legal privileges and economic subsidies. You mean, I asked, that couples involved in homosexual unions are seeking to secure for themselves a variety of benefits which would distinguish them, like married couples, from all other individuals in society? Exactly.

Same-Sex Marriage Does Not Benefit Society

Perhaps she thought she had won the issue by these answers. At any rate, when I asked my next question—that is, why she thought homosexuals should get the same benefits as married couples—she gave me the odd look reserved for slow learners. "Fairness," she decisively answered. It was at this point that I laid my cards on the table. But fairness isn't the issue at all, I said. Of course married heterosexual couples do benefit from the legal status of marriage but to point this out—which, as far as I could tell, was as far as the argument in favor of domestic partnership went—merely begged the question. The point was, why should homosexual partners enjoy these benefits, too?

Or, to put it another way, what is it about married heterosexual couples that make their benefits legitimate? For until supporters of domestic partnership could show that homosexual couples met the same conditions, they could not claim to have been treated unfairly.

And this, of course, is precisely what has not been shown—either by my girlfriend or, more distantly, the policy wonks of the homosexual lobby. To justify giving privileges or exemptions or subsidies to some particular group in society, the benefit of doing so for society at large must first be shown. With heterosexual marriage, the case is clear enough. Heterosexual marriage is a matter of genuine social interest because the family is essential to society's reproduction. The crux of my argument, in other words, was that married couples receive the benefits they do not because the state is interested in promoting romantic love or because the Bible says so or because of the influence of special interest groups but rather because the next generation is something that is and should be of interest to all of us. And, by definition, this is not a case that can be made for homosexual unions. To that degree, the attempt to turn the question of domestic partnership into a debate about fairness falls flat.

The more persistent supporters of domestic partnership will of course respond to this argument by pointing to the case in which homosexual partners adopt children or, in the case of lesbians, undergo artificial insemination. The intention here is to show that the nuclear family is found even among homosexual couples and that, to that extent, homosexual unions do indeed meet the same criterion of social interest as heterosexual ones and thus should be granted legal status. It is a weak argument and one that ultimately back-fires on those who employ it. This is for two reasons. First, adoption by homosexual couples is still exceedingly rare and the law—though many are surprised to learn this—is aimed at the general case. To confer legal benefits on the entire class of would-be homosexual spouses just because some very small minority of this class approximates the pattern of the nuclear family would be a bit like admitting all applicants to a select university on the grounds that a few of them had been shown to meet the entrance requirements.

Only Heterosexual Marriages Are Legitimate

Second, the right of this small minority to the benefits of marriage is dubious in the extreme. Homosexual "families" of whatever type are always and necessarily parasitic on heterosexual ones. In both of these respects, then, the counter-argument from adoption falls well short of its intended mark. Indeed, supporters of domestic partnership who employ this argument inadvertently diminish their case. By accepting that benefits can only be accorded for reasons of social interest, they exclude the overwhelming majority of their constituency—all of those homosexual unions which do not sponsor children—while reaffirming as legitimate the whole range of benefits accorded to heterosexual marriages.

> *"A genuinely public case—one which celebrates the benefits of marriage to society while clearly distinguishing between marriage and other types of relationship—should be made."*

Two years have passed since that Sunday afternoon with my girlfriend and, in those years, the homosexual lobby has gained considerable ground, securing favorable domestic partnership legislation in Hawaii and Vermont and pushing the question of homosexual unions to the forefront of the legislative agenda in a score of other states. Domestic partnership has also gained ground in the private sector. According to the National Gay and Lesbian Task Force, "in 1990, there were less than two dozen companies offering [domestic partnership benefits]. Today, there are more than 2,500." On June 8th, [2000] the nation's three largest auto makers—Chrysler Corp., Ford Motor Company and General Motors Corp.—joined this trend, announcing that from now on employees with same-sex partners would receive the same benefits as married couples.

Observing these developments from the sidelines—perhaps remembering that not very pleasant Sunday two years ago—I seem to find myself defending the unpopular side of the issue more and more frequently. Though the argument of my opponents has remained the same, the tenor of their denials becomes ever more fierce and sanctimonious. Indeed, the perceived justness of domestic partnership legislation seems to have become so well-established that people have intuitions about it. "Though I can't refute you," I've been told more than once, "I know you're wrong." All of which leads me to suspect that the inroads made by the homosexual lobby have not just been in state legislatures and corporate America but in the public conscience as well, which is bad news for those of us on the other side of the issue.

Given the feebleness of the argument in favor of domestic partnership, this is a remarkable development and yet further proof of the cultural left's best-tested strategy: moral exclusion. As the gay lobby would have it, the cause of domestic partnership is firmly within the tradition of the civil rights struggles of the 1960's and '70's. Gay unions, supporters claim, are simply a matter of fairness, of applying the laws of the land equally to everyone. This self-characterization—thoroughly bogus though it is—has two important consequences when allowed to stand unchallenged. In the first place, it allows the homosexual lobby to abrogate to itself all of the pious sentiments so many feel for the civil rights movement. In the second place, it conveniently demonizes their opponents, who—again by virtue of the civil rights analogy—find themselves placed on moral par with George Wallace and the Ku Klux Klan. Not the best platform from which to gain public support.

Sexual Morality Is Not the Issue

Friends of the traditional family do themselves a great disservice by allowing their opponents to set the terms of the debate in this manner. By engaging the homosexual lobby on grounds of sexual morality, not only do they appear politically backwards but, what's worse, they actually assist the left in its effort to cast the pro-family voice in American politics as intolerant and retrograde while representing itself as the virtuous guardian of civil liberties. If the cause of the family is to meet with success in the future, its strategies need to be rethought. In particular, strategists will have to learn a lesson from the left: that the best way to advance the interests of the family is to identify them with the public interest as such.

In the case of the domestic partnership debate, this means that pro-family forces must reject the terms in which the debate has so far been conducted and place the anti-domestic partnership cause on a new footing. To argue that homosexual marriage is sexually immoral will only convince those who already are convinced and alienate the rest, who see such opposition as an attempt to return to the bad old days when fairness wasn't recognized as a political value. Instead, a genuinely public case—one which celebrates the benefits of marriage to society while clearly distinguishing between marriage and other types of relationship—should be made. In this way, traditional family advocates may succeed in shifting the burden of justification to where it should have been all along, squarely on the shoulders of the left. If homosexual marriage becomes a legally recognized fact in the next decade—and it is entirely possible that it will—this will only be because no one has talked about it.

Chapter 2

Should Civil Rights Protections Be Increased?

Chapter Preface

Two *Wall Street Journal* reporters coined the phrase "glass ceiling" in 1986 to describe the invisible barrier that blocks women from advancing to senior positions in organizations, particularly businesses. In the years since 1986, the metaphor of the glass ceiling has also been applied to impediments to minority advancement. Despite the protections extended by the Civil Rights Acts of 1964 and 1991, and the positive effects of affirmative action programs, the glass ceiling still exists for women and minorities. Discrimination in the workplace is one of many issues that seem to call for increased civil rights protections. "The glass ceiling is not only a setback that affects two-thirds of the population, but a serious economic problem that takes a huge financial toll on American business," according to Robert B. Reich, secretary of labor in 1991 and chair of the Glass Ceiling Commission.

The Glass Ceiling Commission was created as part of the Civil Rights Act of 1991 to study and recommend ways to eliminate the barriers faced by women and minorities as they attempt to advance into management positions. The twenty-one-member, bipartisan commission completed its work in 1996 and no longer exists. Many of its recommendations to business—making workplace diversity part of a company's strategic business plan, adopting an affirmative action plan, and expanding executive recruitment to include women and minorities—have been implemented in the public and private sectors. However, the attitudinal barriers and organizational practices that limit opportunity and advancement persist into the twenty-first century, particularly for women.

Experts suggest that the underlying cause for the existence of the glass ceiling is the perception by white males that they as a group are losing competitive advantage, opportunity, and overall control of the workplace as a result of the inclusion of women and minorities. To help protect their positions, the theory goes, white males band together in the workplace to exclude women and minorities from their positions of power. However, minorities and women have made few workplace gains since the beginning of the twenty-first century. For example, a study released in 2002 by the General Accounting Office (GAO) showed that women workers continue to lag behind their male counterparts in advancement and pay. In 1995 a full-time female manager in the communications industry earned eighty-six cents for every dollar earned by a full-time male manager. Five years later, she was earning seventy-three cents for every dollar he earned. Thus, the majority of women managers were actually better off in 1995 than they were in 2000, despite the nation's increasing economic prosperity.

Further study is required to identify the causes of this new-millennium glass ceiling. Some experts suggest that women have been pigeonholed into managerial positions with fewer bonus and stock options. Thus, their compensation did not keep pace with that of male managers. Other researchers contend that the restructuring that took place across and within American industries eliminated many of the lower paid managerial positions that women typically held and replaced them with higher paying positions filled by men. The most recent research (2002), however, suggests an old explanation: When jobs in a given industry become more technical, as most U.S. jobs have, the managerial workforce shifts from women to men. For example, the increased use of computers throughout all industries increased the demand for technological competence in all areas of management, a competence that more men than women have achieved.

Authors in the following chapter examine other areas where activists see a need for greater civil rights protections. Some of the issues they explore include gay and lesbian rights, housing discrimination, slavery reparations, and the employment of disabled Americans.

Current Civil Rights Laws Do Not Adequately Protect Gays and Lesbians

by Matthew Coles

About the author: *Matthew Coles is the director of the Lesbian & Gay Rights Project at the American Civil Liberties Union.*

My name is Matthew Coles. I am the Director of the Lesbian & Gay Rights Project at the American Civil Liberties Union. I am here for my ACLU colleagues from across the nation, and for my colleagues at Lambda Legal Defense and Education Fund, Gay and Lesbian Advocates and Defenders and the National Center for Lesbian Rights.

We are the lawyers who handle most of the cases involving discrimination against lesbians, gay men and bisexuals. We are the people who represent the X-Ray technician in eastern Washington who never knew a day of peace at work and was eventually hounded out of her job by a supervisor who hated her because she was, in his words, "a faggot." We are the people who represent the shoe factory worker in Maine who, as the federal appeals court in Boston put it, "toiled in a wretchedly hostile environment," before he lost his job. We are the people who represent an inspirational choral teacher in Alabama, who thought until the day he was fired that he'd successfully kept his family life private, and whose students begged the school board to bring him back. We are the people who represent the championship volleyball coach, the hard working accountant, the talented young lawyer, the world weary mechanic, and on and on and on, all of whom learned to their shock that the American promise that talent and hard work are what matter was, for them at least, an empty promise.

There is little that we can do for most of those people. If they work for government, they can claim limited protection under the constitution, and sometimes under civil service. In 12 states, they are fully protected by civil rights laws that prohibit discrimination based on sexual orientation. But if like most

Matthew Coles, testimony before the U.S. Senate Committee on Health, Education, Labor, and Pensions Hearing on the Employment Non-Discrimination Act, Washington, DC, February 27, 2002.

Americans, they work for private businesses in the other 38 states, they are just out of luck.

But those people we represent are the tip of the iceberg. For most lesbian/gay Americans, survival comes down to this: separate the two most important parts of your life, work and family, so that neither ever knows anything about the other. And then pray that you never slip up.

ENDA Provides Simple Justice

Imagine making certain there is no trace of the most important person in your life where you work; imagine not just that she or he never appears there, but that no one who works there can ever be allowed to know she or he exists. Imagine knowing that you risk your career if you slip and mention her name, much less casually say what she thought of the show you saw on TV last night. Imagine that your future depends on no one knowing that you are married, or that you hang around with other people who are married, or go to places where married people go. Now imagine that you have to keep this up. For good. It is a balancing act that exacts a price in human emotion that is terrifying.

The answer, for both the people we represent and the vast numbers who protect themselves by splitting their lives apart, is the bill you have before you. ENDA [the Employment Non-Discrimination Act] provides what simple justice demands; that no one should lose a job because of who they are.[1] For the people we represent and others like them, it offers a remedy. For the rest, it provides a promise that denying family is not the price of having work.

While the remedy is important, it is that promise that matters most. Civil rights laws work not because we are able to haul those who disobey them to court, but because most Americans are good, law abiding people. When we say that as a nation that no one should lose a job because of religion, most businesses accept that.

> *"A law against sexual orientation discrimination says that we really believe the American promise that every one should have a fair chance."*

Most people accept it because our laws are above all, a statement about what we believe as a people. So too with a law against sexual orientation discrimination. And what we say with a federal civil rights law banning employment discrimination based on sexual orientation is not that we endorse being gay, or being heterosexual, any more than our federal civil rights laws against religious discrimination endorse being Christian, or Jewish or Muslim or agnostic. A law against sexual orientation discrimination says that we really believe the American promise that every one should have a fair chance to go where their brains and guts and grit can take them. A law against sexual orientation discrimination says that we really

1. As of February 11, 2003, the ENDA was still in Congress.

believe in that promise, and that we want it to be real. That isn't much, and yet it is everything.

The X-Ray technician in Washington, the shoe worker in Maine, the choral teacher in Alabama, and those silent thousands, they all need the promise. We all need a federal law banning employment discrimination based on sexual orientation and we need it now.

Housing Discrimination Persists Despite Fair Housing Laws

by Eleanor Novek

About the author: *Eleanor Novek is a professor of communications at Monmouth University. She conducts research on the role of communication in the persistence of racial residential segregation.*

In *Race in America: The Struggle for Equality*, Patricia J. Williams, a legal scholar, recalls seeing an advertisement for a two-bedroom apartment in Madison, Wisconsin. The landlord agreed to meet her at the address to show the place. Williams, who is African-American, arrived first. "I saw her catch sight of me as I sat on the doorstep. I saw her walk slower and slower, squinting at me as I sat in the sunshine. At ten minutes after three, I was back in my car driving away without having seen the apartment. The woman had explained to me that a 'terrible mistake' had occurred, that the apartment had been rented without her knowledge . . ."

Williams's experience is a common one for people of color in all walks of life. Decades after the passage of federal fair housing laws, housing discrimination and racial segregation are alive and well in the United States. Many communities still operate under a strict "virtual apartheid," and in some parts of the country, racially divided neighborhoods are even more prevalent than they were before civil rights legislation. Extensive regional and national studies have documented that minority home seekers receive less assistance than whites in finding housing that meets their needs and are more likely to be turned down for mortgage loans and home insurance than comparably qualified white applicants. Buyers of all races continue to be steered toward neighborhoods where their own ethnic groups are concentrated.

While many ethnic groups have encountered housing discrimination, no group has experienced the sustained high level of residential segregation that has been imposed on African Americans. Segregation has concentrated African Americans into disadvantaged neighborhoods characterized by higher crime rates, fewer public services, and lower housing values. It has restricted their access to job opportunities, information resources and political influence. Schools in segregated areas are plagued by high dropout rates and severe educational disparities that threaten the life chances of African-American children. Racial residential segregation is a primary cause of urban poverty and inequality in the United States.

Although many forces are responsible for this persistence of racial segregation, the role of communication is often overlooked. Since passage of the Fair Housing Act, polite social interaction is often used to carry the same ugly messages formerly stated directly, with entire conversations conducted as if something other than race is causing the denial of housing. These communication strategies have helped to preserve segregation where the law has tried to dismantle it.

History of Residential Segregation

Scholars track the institutionalization of racial separation to the early 1900s, when large numbers of blacks migrated from the rural South in search of factory jobs. When they tried to settle in the largely white urban areas of the North and the Midwest, they met with exclusion, intimidation and violence.

Whites in some cities boycotted and harassed businesses like boarding houses, hotels, and real estate firms that provided shelter to African Americans. Other whites established suburbs where they used zoning laws and exclusionary deeds to keep out people of color. Responding to these dynamics, real estate agents found it easiest and most profitable to steer home buyers and renters to neighborhoods where people of their own races were already concentrated.

Such steering was soon underscored by federal policies. In the 1930s and '40s, the Federal Housing Administration underwrote mortgages in segregated white neighborhoods, while directing lenders to turn down minority mortgages. Between 1930 and 1960, fewer than 1 percent of all mortgages in the nation were issued to African Americans. In the 1960s, urban renewal plans placed low-income housing projects in minority neighborhoods, concentrating the nation's poorest residents in the same neighborhoods occupied by people of color.

The Federal Fair Housing Act of 1968 outlawed overtly discriminatory market practices like exclusionary deeds, steering and redlining, but it had relatively little effect on established routines among real estate agents and lenders. Over the next two decades, despite increases in income, education and job status for minorities, housing patterns remained segregated. In the 1990s, despite modest changes in newer suburban neighborhoods in the South and West, segregation actually deepened in many cities. Between 1996 and 1998, the U.S. Department of Justice prosecuted more than 80 cases of criminal interference with housing rights, including cross-burnings, shootings and fire-bombings.

Biased Brokers

Such acts of violence are not the primary way that segregation is reinforced in much of the country, however. Real estate sales and rental agents, mortgage lenders and insurers all have significant influence on the choices home buyers make. And despite the Fair Housing Act, race still influences their interactions with their customers.

First, there is direct discrimination. Minority home buyers receive less assistance than whites in finding housing that meets their needs, and are more likely to be turned down or overcharged for home loans and insurance than comparably qualified white applicants. Doug Massey and Nancy Denton describe in *American Apartheid: Segregation and the Making of the Underclass* how racial minority customers are told that the unit they want to see has just been sold or rented, or they are shown only one advertised unit and told that no others are available.

At some real estate offices, Massey and Denton note, minority customers are "told that the selling agents are too busy and to come back later; their phone number may be taken but a return call never made; they may be shown units but offered no assistance in arranging financing; or they may be treated brusquely and discourteously in hopes that they will leave" National studies using matched pairs of testers have documented these actions at real estate firms and mortgage lenders around the country. Many of these abuses originate in the earliest personal interactions between sellers and buyers, or in the first informational materials home buyers confront.

Less directly abusive, but even more clearly perpetuating segregation is the practice of steering, whereby customers are strongly encouraged, both by what they are shown and by "commentary," to buy or rent in single-race neighborhoods where they "fit in." When consumers want to inspect housing in locations where they would be in a racial minority, some real estate agents try to discourage them through conversation. In Bloomington, IN, an agent warned an Asian woman and her white husband away from a house they wanted to buy because it was not in "a mixed neighborhood." And a white woman in Ocean, NJ was assured by an agent that "this is a great neighborhood—there are none of them here." Real estate salespeople often say they know other agents who discuss the racial makeup of neighborhoods with clients, but they refuse to discuss such practices in detail, fearful of backlash from those agents.

> *"Decades after the passage of the federal fair housing laws, housing discrimination and racial segregation are alive and well in the United States."*

Research demonstrates that white buyers typically hear positive comments from agents praising neighborhoods and schools in mostly white areas, but they hear discouraging comments about neighborhood amenities and schools when a neighborhood's population is more than 30 percent black. Black customers tend to hear little commentary—positive or negative—from agents about predominantly black neighborhoods, but they are invariably warned against buying in predominantly white areas because of the possible "trouble" they would face there.

Advertising Exclusivity

Newspaper real estate ads are a key source of information for home seekers, and they often contain discriminatory messages. The Federal Fair Housing Act forbids references to race, color, religion, sex, handicap, familial status or national origin in real estate advertising, but subtler messages of exclusion in photographs or text often get through. In some real estate markets, for example, the models shown in photographic ads for homes and apartment complexes are all white, and very blonde. Some have described neighborhoods "where Wally and the Beaver would feel right at home," or homes built in "the style of Northern Europe," available only to "a select few" or representing "a return to family values."

These tactics have resulted in individual complaints and lawsuits. Some courts have ruled that using only white models in real estate advertisements sends a discriminatory message to other races. In one study, African-American and white respondents viewed groups of real estate ads with white models only and with a mix of black and white models. Typical responses to the all-white ads included: "Because the 'actors' are perceived to be all Europeans, I would question if African Americans would be welcome here," and "From people pictured on posters, this apartment complex is 'for white only.'"

In 1993, in partial settlement of a lawsuit, The *New York Times* began requiring that real estate ads containing photos of people be representative of the racial makeup in the New York metropolitan area. Some advertisers responded by removing all human figures from their ads. In 1994, the publishers of the *Philadelphia Inquirer* and the *Philadelphia Daily News* cautioned advertisers not to use "coded" text in ads, including "such words and phrases as traditional, prestigious, established and private community, which, when used in a certain context, could be interpreted to convey racial exclusivity."

Data Labeling

Internet marketing sites and the practice of computer-assisted target marketing have added a new twist to communication about race and real estate. Many residential sales firms, including brands like Century 21 and Re/MAX, have established consumer web sites to attract customers, offering prospective home buyers information and advice from mortgage rates to moving tips. Some sites furnish "neighborhood profile" services, where consumers can type in the street address or zip code of a home and receive a description of nearby schools, crime rates, and property values. Or they may offer "neighborhood matching," a service that allows relocating buyers to type in the zip codes of their current neighborhoods and find communities in other cities with comparably priced housing.

The demographic information on Internet real estate sites is provided by marketing services such as Lysias, Taconic Data, CACI Marketing Systems and Claritas. These firms combine demographic data from the U.S. Census with consumer spending research and package the information for easy use by commercial clients. Such firms pioneered "cluster marketing" techniques in the 1980s, analyzing the consumer habits of neighborhoods across the U.S. by zip code and then assigning them catchy nicknames like "Affluent Suburbia," "Mid-City Mix," and "Metro Singles."

However, some of these profiles categorize neighborhoods not only by zip code and consumer behavior, but also by ethnic signifiers. For example, a profile offered by CACI Marketing Systems characterized one zip code as having mostly black residents who had not completed high school and "tend to purchase fast food and takeout food from chicken restaurants." Claritas' online "Hispanic Mix" neighborhood profile is decorated with a cartoon image of a brown-skinned mother shopping at a sidewalk market, and

> *"Since passage of the Fair Housing Act, polite social interaction is often used to carry the same ugly messages formerly stated directly."*

describes residents who are pro basketball fans and use money orders to pay their bills.

MicroVision's middle-income "City Ties" cluster (where residents are said to eat at chicken restaurants, smoke menthol cigarettes, and read *Ebony* magazine) is illustrated by a photo of a smiling black family with three children. Its upscale "Metro Singles" cluster (where residents are said to use sunburn remedies and have dental insurance) is illustrated by a blonde white woman reclining alone on a sofa.

In February 1999, the National Association of Realtors took a stand against the use of racial and ethnic demographic information on members' real estate websites, but a number of firms continue the practice. These techniques have recently come under fire from community groups and citizens. ACORN, a non-profit fair housing organization, has charged Wells Fargo/Norwest Mortgage with racial discrimination over the company's Internet real estate site (which has since been taken down). Plaintiffs argued that the website's neighborhood profiles used "overt racial classifications" to discourage people from inspecting or buying homes in predominantly minority areas by exaggerating the desirability of areas deemed white occupied and the drawbacks of areas classified as minority occupied. The plaintiffs also claim the site's neighborhood matching feature steered residents of predominantly minority zip codes to other minority zip codes, and referred residents of predominantly white zip codes to other white zip codes.

The practices described above are common but hard to track, located more often by anecdotal example than by research. Although they are not as dramatic as acts of violence and not as quantifiable as redlining, they play a significant role in the persistence of housing discrimination. Together, they may be as discouraging to the growth of integrated communities as the easier-to-measure practices of discriminatory pricing, mortgage lending and insurance underwriting. However, these habits that support segregation can be broken by a concerted effort to bring them into the light of day. . . .

First, let's talk about what is going on. The absence of public dialogue is one of the conditions that allow racial discrimination to persist. Most individual home buyers see themselves not as change agents but as consumers whose decisions are merely individual choices that have no broader impact. Community organizations and coalitions play a key role in helping to raise public awareness of segregation and the contemporary problems it creates.

Second, community organizations can strengthen their case by partnering with researchers and journalists to more precisely document the scope of residential segregation in their communities. Academic researchers can teach local groups techniques for tracing social patterns and analyzing their impact in a community over time. Journalists can bring the issue of segregation to public attention. Rather than focusing their stories on individual acts of housing bias involving a few people, news organizations need to cover residential segregation as an issue story, highlighting the social processess and outcomes that affect thousands of people. Such efforts can begin to raise broader public support for changes in policy. Publishers and editors should also assess the racially exclusive advertising practices in their own real estate sections and pressure advertisers to change.

Finally, we must call on public officials at local, state and federal levels to address residential segregation through assertive social programs. Models for these already exist, such as the one developed by the Fund for an Open Society in Philadelphia. This plan calls for the creation of neighborhood enterprise zones dedicated to residential integration. It suggests the creation of mortgage subsidies and tax exemptions for homeowners, and recommends that participating localities be made eligible for dedicated funding for new construction and school support. The Fair Share Housing Center in Cherry Hill, NJ works with residents of Mt. Laurel, NJ to develop low-income housing that would allow some of Camden's inner city residents to afford suburban housing. The South Orange/Maplewood Community Coalition on Race is also testing out some of these ideas.

Segregation is a stubborn problem. Although some communication practices have been used to circumvent fair housing and integration, others can help. Let's talk frankly about the racial makeup of our neighborhoods. Let's document and publicize what is going on. Let's define segregation as a social harm rather than as an inconvenient byproduct of individual preferences. And let's come up with alternatives for viable communities with quality of life for all.

Reparations for African American Slavery Are Necessary for the Advancement of Civil Rights

by Jeffrey Ghannam

About the author: *Jeffrey Ghannam is a legal affairs writer for the* ABA Journal, *the monthly publication of the American Bar Association.*

For years, Gwendolyn Midlo Hall pored over handwritten French, Spanish and English slave documents in a massive effort to document Afro-Louisiana history.

With stunning authority, she untangled a history of African slave names, genders, ages, occupations, illnesses, family relationships, ethnicity, places of origin, prices paid by slave owners, slaves' testimony and emancipations.

A few mouse clicks provide computer access to the product of Hall's work, Databases for the Study of Afro-Louisiana History and Genealogy 1699–1860. The CD-ROM from Louisiana State University Press, which she edited, offers insight into the inhumanity of slavery.

"Look, this is unique and it shows which masters owned which slaves and how much they cost," says Hall, a former Rutgers University history professor who is now a researcher and writer in New Orleans. "And there is a way of calculating precisely which fortunes were made by which families."

As she worked compiling the records, Hall came to the realization that her work could have implications far beyond adding to the historical portrait of slavery. The documents also provide a factual basis that may give rise to legal claims for reparations by the descendants of Louisiana's African slaves.

"I started it for my own purposes as a historian," Hall says. "As time went by, I realized that this does have implications for the reparations issue."

In the growing debate over whether African-Americans are entitled to some form of redress for the wrongs committed against their ancestors who were brought to America as slaves, Hall's databases will figure prominently. The issue gains added urgency as time goes by and the documents become more scarce.

> *"Until America's white ruling class accepts the fact that the book never closes on massive, unredressed social wrongs, America can have no future as one people."*

To the activists, lawyers and politicians who are laying the moral, legal and political groundwork on the issue, reparations can mean many things. Some want an apology for the 246-year practice of slavery in America. Some propose a presidential commission to inquire into the need and extent of possible monetary relief, while others want corporations to make restitution for helping to maintain slavery.

Those waging the campaign for reparations or restitution, depending upon what is being sought, have been documenting, strategizing and promoting the cause on a national basis.

Earlier this year [2000], Chicago became the fifth major U.S. city to endorse federal hearings on reparations. Other cities are considering or have paid reparations in connection with race riots in the past. In Africa last year [1999], Benin and Ghana apologized for their nations' historic roles in the slave trade.

A simple resolution of the reparations question is not expected. Those who press the issue build on black efforts for recompense that began soon after the Civil War ended. They also look to the precedents of legislative recompense and legal settlements for other ethnic, religious and racial minorities around the world.

Setting a Precedent

The activists point to the example of Japanese-Americans, interned during World War II, who received an apology and compensation from the U.S. government in 1988. They note that Holocaust survivors will receive billions of dollars in settlements paid by the Germans and the Swiss.

They argue that the United States owes African-Americans for their ancestors' vast contributions to building the nation's public and private wealth, as well as for the legacy of discrimination that persists despite constitutional and legislative attempts to eliminate it.

But can the Holocaust settlements be a model for African-American reparations?

"Yes and no," says Michael Hausfeld, a Washington, D.C., lawyer who has handled Holocaust litigation. "Yes, with respect to part of what was sought was a historical reckoning and acknowledgment that an offense against humanity was committed, and that there were victims of that offense who received no justice."

No, he says, in that Holocaust settlements were brought on behalf of direct survivors—the actual victims.

"To that extent, there is a greater proximity of the wrong to the individual," Hausfeld says. "When you have many generations from the offense it becomes almost impossible to fashion an appropriate remedy as a relief."

Hausfeld says that the challenge with African-Americans' reparations claims is the inability to translate the true nature of the injury into damages suffered.

"In my judgment, you can never equate a precise calculated amount for being enslaved," he says. "To say, 'Here's $4.20 that you would have earned,' 100 years later, it really diminishes what had occurred."

But that does not necessarily make the moral wrong any less real, even for those who cannot trace their ancestry directly back to slaves.

Moreover, Hausfeld says, sources like Hall's databases confront those who have yet to acknowledge their roles in contributing to the system of slavery.

"Even if it can't be reduced to a calculable form of compensation," Hausfeld says, "the fact that you have such a large body of identifiable entities that have escaped any accountability is a poor message for morality and inhumanity in the future."

Europe and America Inflicted Damage

To Randall Robinson, the impact of slavery persists to this day. In a book published [in 2000], *The Debt: What America Owes to Blacks*, he writes that Europe and America inflicted unimaginable horrors on Africa and its people. Europe not only paid no compensation to Africa but went on to remap the continent for economic exploitation.

"It is a human rights crime without parallel in the modern world," writes Robinson, founder and president of TransAfrica, a lobbying group based in Washington, D.C. "For it produces its victims *ad infinitum*, long after the active stage of the crime has ended."

Robinson, whose book has informed the dialogue on African-American reparations, writes that he knows of no statute of limitations—either legal or moral—that would extinguish claims.

"Until America's white ruling class accepts the fact that the book never closes on massive, unredressed social wrongs, America can have no future as one people," he writes. "Questions

> *"You have a problem that cries out across history. . . . What I'm trying to do is make this a healing, to get the past behind us."*

must be raised to American private, as well as public, institutions. Which American families and institutions, for instance, were endowed in perpetuity by the commerce of slavery? What is a fair measure of restitution for this, the most important of all American human rights abuses?"

Like other reparations proponents, Robinson advances the legal theory of unjust enrichment to seek recovery for the benefits slave laborers bestowed on the nation. That theory is upheld by international law, he says.

Robinson notes in his book that President Abraham Lincoln supported a plan during the Civil War to compensate slave owners for their loss of "property." But his successor, President Andrew Johnson, vetoed legislation that would have compensated ex-slaves, as well.

There would be no 40 acres and no mule.[1]

Troubling Trail

Tracing the harm to individuals may be impossible for many African-Americans outside of Hall's databases. Still, some succeed.

Building a case for reparations was not Percy Pierre's intent when he set out to trace his ancestry 20 years ago. Coming from a close-knit family, he says, it was important to rediscover his history.

Pierre of East Lansing, Mich., used Hall's databases to discover an ancestor who hailed from Mozambique. She was the grandmother of a great-great-grandfather, a slave in Louisiana who took the surname Pierre.

> *"These three words—I am sorry—are a foundation for beginning again . . . for restoring lost trust, and a necessary first step in moving forward constructively."*

"I could lay it out as a legal argument," says Pierre, a professor of electrical engineering at Michigan State University who grew up in Louisiana. "If I want to go back and document unpaid labor by my ancestors, I can."

For two years, he devoted two days a week to tracing his ancestry to his great-great-grandfather. "I can document who owned him, how long he was a slave," Pierre says. "I can produce papers where a value was put on him as a slave. I can do that for probably 20 of my ancestors, and I can identify the families who owned them. I can identify their descendants. I can trace their property, what happened to their plantation. It's doable. I'm absolutely sure."

Building a link to his family past remains key to Pierre's efforts. "On a personal level, that's what it's about," he says. "It's about family." But the legal dimension exists. "It's there."

Tracing the money is key for Richard America, a professor at Georgetown University in Washington, D.C., who says there should be an accounting of what was taken from African-Americans.

"Slavery and discrimination were mechanisms for transferring money wrongfully" from blacks to whites, says America, author of a forthcoming book, *Solv-*

---

1. A reference to the plan to give freed slaves forty acres of farmland and a mule as compensation for their labor as slaves.

ing the Race Problem. "So reparations are a way of capturing the unjust enrichment that whites have today."

He advocates public policies redirecting that wealth to blacks in the form of grants for housing, businesses and education. "Money was taken away," America says. "That's the heart of the problem in a nutshell."

Reparations Are a Legitimate Remedy

Many in the pro-reparations camp believe the United States is a country willing to make amends.

"Many of us work hard to make it clear that we do not deny that reparations should have been paid to Japanese-Americans," says Adjoa Aiyetoro, legal counsel for the National Coalition of Blacks for Reparations in America. Based in Washington, D.C., N'COBRA is an umbrella for more than two dozen groups seeking to advance the campaign for reparations.

"We don't want to get into a competitive thing—'Why them and not us?'" Aiyetoro says. "It underscores that reparations are a legitimate form of remedy. It shows the United States recognizes the issue."

Aiyetoro notes that N'COBRA helped move the reparations issue into the mainstream in the early 1990s.

Among those advancing the cause are black intellectuals, including Harvard law professor Charles J. Ogletree, who admits to publicly joining an effort only recently that grassroots activists initiated decades ago.

Ogletree is coordinating a national effort to study legal strategies and legislative alternatives to support reparations. Specifically, he wants to address "the consistent and deep-seated problems we have in terms of health care, employment and housing."

But he adds that the inquiry is in its early stages and must consider many points of view on the issue.

The International Approach

Robert Brock, a Washington, D.C., legal activist for 45 years and president of the Self Determination Committee, a reparations lobbying group, has been thinking about the issue for a long time. He argues that international law provides a basis for claims to reparations because blacks were brought to these shores in captivity, and that their legal claims survive the passage of time.

"I trace it all the way to the first act," he says. "You have to have a war before you capture me. War is an international act, isn't it? Slavery is an international act, isn't it? Captivity is an international act over the high seas three miles out of African territory.

"Blacks touched the United States by being brought here without a passport, immigration papers and consent," Brock says. "But they were brought over the ocean, which is admiralty law. Admiralty law is international law. Blacks' rights lie in international law."

Brock argues that the war against African slaves and their descendants ended with passage of the 13th Amendment in 1865. So before the 100-year anniversary of the amendment, he filed a class action complaint against the United States in Los Angeles federal court. He sought reparations and $500,000 in damages, plus interest, for each African-American.

"I did that with the effect of stopping the statute of limitations," Brock maintains. "How many people know about that? Very few. Now their right to get reparations for slave labor is continued."

The government never responded, he says.

Rep. John Conyers, D-Mich., has introduced a bill in the House each year since 1989 calling for the president to appoint a commission to study reparations.

"We're not trying to strike a 'who had slaves and who did not' inquiry," Conyers says. "You have a problem that cries out across history for some kind of enlightened and compassionate resolution. What I'm trying to do is make this a healing, to get the past behind us. This matter is not going to be whisked away."

If created, the commission would seek answers to fundamental questions: Is an apology due? Should reparations be paid? To whom and in what form? The bill, H.R. 40, which has limited bipartisan support, languishes in the House Judiciary Committee.

Appeal Is Back by Legal and Moral Authority

"People say it's too late or costs too much," Conyers says. "Some suggest that we're taking the victims' approach. But, of course, we already are victims. We're not approaching it as victims. We seek justice, and we're trying to figure out how to do it."

He says the Holocaust settlements are proof that the African-American appeal is backed by legal and moral authority, that reparations aren't some extra-legal remedy that belongs to the past but a process that is the usual means to resolve harms done by a nation against a people.

When Rep. Tony P. Hall, D-Ohio introduced in June [2000] the Apology for Slavery Resolution of 2000, H. Con. Res. 356, he told reporters that apologizing is humbling. "These three words—'I am sorry'—are a foundation for beginning again, a small price to pay for restoring lost trust, and a necessary first step in moving forward constructively."

Hall says the apology would build on the precedents that Congress set when it apologized to Japanese-Americans and to Native Hawaiians for the role the United States played in the overthrow of the Kingdom of Hawaii in the 1890s. An apology would constitute official government policy.

Like Conyers' bill, Hall's calls for a commission to study slavery's legacy, and it supports a national museum and memorial, which are included in similar proposals by Reps. John Lewis, D-Ga., and Cliff Stearns, R-Fla.

And, also like Conyers' bill, Hall's resolution sits in the House Judiciary Committee. "No hearings. No vote. No nothing," says Max Finberg, Hall's legislative assistant. "That tells us it's probably not going anywhere."

> *"Until and unless this country and its leadership and its people deal straight up with actually making reparations, we're not going to have racial healing."*

Deadria Farmer-Paellmann of New York City also has encountered frustrations in a campaign for justice. Her efforts rest on the theory that some corporations should make restitution to African-Americans for their roles in maintaining slave labor.

Farmer-Paellmann, a graduate of New England School of Law in Boston, began her law studies with the intention of finding a case for reparations. She says she is close. In the meantime, she is targeting companies that benefited from slavery. An economy supported by slave labor helped companies prosper, and restitution can be claimed based on unjust enrichment, she says.

"Once all is said and done, you will see a list of companies that touch on every aspect of corporate life in America," she says. "Americans of all races will be more educated about what slaves did for this country. We were there in every aspect of American business life."

Farmer-Paellmann has so far approached Aetna, the Hartford, Conn.-based insurance giant, and asked for an apology for its role in helping to maintain slavery by writing life insurance policies on slaves with their owners as beneficiaries.

Aetna apologized for writing what it says were five slave policies just after the company's 1853 founding, says spokesman Fred Laberge. The policies covered short periods of time, such as planting season. "In the year 2000, it sounds terrible to have done something like that," Laberge says. "Today we express our regret at being a part of this."

Diversity Is Not the Answer

But Aetna plans no further action, he says. The company addresses today's needs, he says, with a minority internship program, corporate scholarship funding and diversity initiatives. "The company has a track record of being a very diverse, open place today."

But Farmer-Paellmann is not satisfied. "Their diversity policy has a lot to do with the fact that they needed one, and the charitable programs still do not address the debts that they owe," she says. "They're giving gifts; they're not paying a debt."

She would like to see, for instance, the creation of a trust to help descendants of African slaves establish their own businesses. "The idea is to become a part of the business world in America," she says. "I'm looking for us to not have to rely on programs and to become more economically independent."

Ambivalence that cuts across racial lines hovers over the reparations issue.

Reaction from the white community, according to legislative assistant Finberg, includes views that the civil rights movement and desegregation resolved issues of inequality. A common refrain is that many blacks are successful in business, entertainment and sports.

Rep. Henry Hyde, R-Ill., chairman of the House Judiciary Committee, did not return phone calls seeking comment on the reparations issue. But several years ago, he said, "I never owned a slave. I never oppressed anybody. I don't know that I should have to pay for someone who did [own slaves] generations before I was born."

Ambivalent Attitudes

Many in the African-American community have not taken a position on reparations. They wonder whether an apology would be enough and whether it would be meaningless without reparations. Many refuse to get their hopes up for either.

The Rev. Carl Baldwin of Godian Fellowship Mission in New York City is the grandson of a slave. He has been an activist since his days in Birmingham, Ala., where he took part in some of the early civil rights sit-ins. He supports reparations but doesn't expect to see them in his lifetime. "There are those who say we should get millions," Baldwin says of his parishioners. "There are those who say we should let it drop."

Finberg says he has heard from various sides in the debate and believes some members of the black community are not ready to forgive whites for slavery. "And letting them off for all the offenses that have been heaped upon [the black community] with a simple apology" doesn't cut it, Finberg says. Meanwhile, many black members of Congress have shied away from the idea of an apology, he says. "They have a lot of battles to fight in overcoming racial discrimination, and it's not one that they choose to invest their energy in."

Pierre wants acknowledgment for contributions blacks made during slavery. He points to Southern plantations that inform tourists about the lives of the owners but fail to reveal the stories of the slaves who built and supported the estates. "My attitude is that we should not forget that," he says. "We ought to tell that story."

Finberg says Rep. Hall does not support government-paid cash reparations for every African-American "at this stage." Instead, he supports building a museum to address the historical record and developing school curriculums to more accurately discuss slavery.

To Ogletree, "The idea is not to build a monument or get a check but to change the quality of care of those who are still suffering from centuries-old problems of segregation, bigotry and lack of meaningful opportunity."

He finds the idea of individual monetary restitution in the form of checks sent to African-Americans "a cheap form of forgiveness and an insult to those millions of Africans who lost their lives to the slave trade."

But whatever final form reparations might take, conviction is growing that the campaign cannot let up.

"You have to plug along and make it an issue that people cannot ignore," says activist Aiyetoro. "Until and unless this country and its leadership and its people deal straight up with actually making reparations, we're not going to have racial healing."

Disabled Workers Need Better Protection from Employment Discrimination

by Thomas DeLeire

About the author: *Thomas DeLeire is an assistant professor at the Harris Graduate School of Public Policy Studies at the University of Chicago.*

Economists commonly lament public policies that transfer resources to a particular group because such policies ignore the "law of unintended consequences." Economists point out, for example, that the law of unintended consequences is at work when workers' wages fall in response to a mandated increase in benefits or when employment falls in response to an increase in the minimum wage. As Henry Hazlitt said in *Economics in One Lesson*, "Depth in economics consists in looking for all the consequences of a policy instead of merely resting one's gaze on those immediately visible."

The employment provisions of the Americans with Disabilities Act (ADA) exemplify the law of unintended consequences because those provisions have *harmed* the intended beneficiaries of the Act, not helped them. ADA was enacted to remove barriers to employment of people with disabilities by banning discrimination and requiring employers to accommodate disabilities (e.g., by providing a magnified computer screen for a vision-impaired person). However, studies of the consequences of the employment provisions of ADA show that the Act has led to less employment of disabled workers.

Why has ADA harmed its intended beneficiaries? The added cost of employing disabled workers to comply with the accommodation mandate of ADA has made those workers relatively unattractive to firms. Moreover, the threats of prosecution by the Equal Employment Opportunity Commission (EEOC) and litigation by disabled workers, both of which were to have deterred firms from

Thomas DeLeire, "The Unintended Consequences of the Americans with Disabilities Act," *Regulation: The Cato Review of Business and Government*, vol. 23, 2000, pp. 21–24. Copyright © 2000 by the Cato Institute. All rights reserved. Reproduced by permission.

shedding their disabled workforce, have in fact led firms to avoid hiring some disabled workers in the first place.

That result is not surprising to students of economics. After all, if you raise the price of a good or service, you must expect that less of it will be bought. Likewise, theories of labor demand predict that when a group of workers becomes more expensive, firms will hire other workers or substitute capital for labor.

The Intended Beneficiaries of ADA

Disabled Americans are a large and economically disadvantaged group. In 1995, according to the Survey of Income and Program Participation (a nationally representative survey that queries individuals about their disability and employment status), 11.6 percent of men and women in the working-age population (ages 18 to 65) reported a health impairment that limited either the type or amount of work they could do. That percentage has been rising: in 1986, for example, 9.6 percent of the working-age population reported a disability.

We commonly think of the intended beneficiaries of ADA as persons with mobility, vision, or hearing impairments. ADA, however, covers a vast number of health impairments. The Act defines a disability as "a physical or mental impairment that substantially limits one or more major life activities, a record of such an impairment, [or] being regarded as having such an impairment." Major life activities include walking, lifting, seeing, hearing, breathing, and—most importantly for the employment provisions of ADA—working. In fact, mobility, vision, and hearing impairments represent merely 17 percent of the population of men with disabilities. By far the most prevalent of disabilities reported in surveys are bad backs and heart disease. Thus, ADA covers many more people than those commonly thought of as disabled. On the other hand, the disabled who are most often portrayed in newspaper articles about the excesses of ADA—the mentally disabled and substance abusers—represent only 6.7 percent of the disabled population.

As a group, people with disabilities earn less than people without disabilities. Despite receiving government-provided benefits, people with disabilities have relatively low incomes. The average annual income (including government transfers) of disabled men was only 61 percent of that of

> *"Studies of the consequences of the employment provisions of the ADA [Americans with Disabilities Act] show that the Act has led to less employment of disabled workers."*

nondisabled men in 1992, and labor earnings of disabled men averaged only 47 percent of the earnings of nondisabled men.

These differences in earnings are explained partly by the fact that fewer people with disabilities work: only 53 percent of disabled men work compared with 89 percent of nondisabled men. However, disabled workers also receive lower pay when they do work; their average wage is only 79 percent of the average wage of nondisabled workers. In addition, people with disabilities often are additionally disadvantaged in that they are generally less educated, older, and employed in less-skilled occupations than are the nondisabled.

The fact that disabled people work less and earn less when they work is consistent with the view that people with disabilities face barriers in the labor market. The same fact is also consistent with the (almost tautological) view that a disability reduces a person's productivity.

How ADA Works

The employment mandates of ADA have two broad goals. One goal, which is similar to that of other civil rights legislation, is to ensure that people with disabilities have access to types of employment from which they traditionally have been excluded. The second goal, which is similar to that of antipoverty programs, is to increase job opportunities for disabled people. Therefore, the employment provisions of ADA consist of two parts:

• Section 101(8) prohibits wage and employment discrimination against "qualified individuals with a disability." A qualified individual with a disability is "an individual with a disability who, with or without reasonable accommodation, can perform the essential functions of the employment position."

• Section 101(9) requires an employer to provide a "reasonable accommodation"—a change in the work environment that results in an equal employment opportunity for a person with a disability.

> "The cost of complying with the Act may have reduced the demand for disabled workers and thereby . . . undone ADA's intended effects."

To meet the reasonable accommodation provision of Section 101(9), an employer may be required to modify facilities, redefine jobs, revise work schedules, provide special equipment or assistance, give training or other forms of support, or eliminate nonessential job functions. A business can avoid an accommodation only if it would cause "undue hardship" to the nature or operation of the business.

The mandates of the ADA have a major effect on employment decisions because of the costs they can impose. Section 101(9) is a significant element of ADA's employment provisions because providing reasonable accommodations can be costly for employers. Unfortunately, there is little evidence about the costs of accommodation. The evidence at hand comes from the President's Job Accommodation Network (JAN) and studies of federal contractors under the Rehabilitation Act of 1974, such as the study conducted by Berkeley Planning Associates (BPA) in 1982. JAN reports that the median accommodation under ADA costs $500 or less. The BPA study found that the average cost of an accommodation is very low—approximately $900—and that 51 percent of accommodations cost nothing.

In spite of such results, it would be wrong to conclude that ADA has little effect on employers. First, both sources underestimate the costs of accommodation by including only monetary costs. Allowing a disabled employee to work a more flexible schedule, for example, might not increase a firm's out-of-pocket expenses, but it does increase a firm's costs.

> *"Substantial barriers to the employment of people with disabilities persist in spite of the employment mandates of ADA."*

Second, the burden of ADA is not the less-expensive accommodations that very likely would have been made even in the absence of a government mandate but rather the more expensive ones. According to JAN, 12 percent of accommodations cost more than $2,000 and 4 percent cost more than $5,000. The BPA study found that 8 percent of accommodations cost more than $2,000, 4 percent of accommodations cost more than $5,000, and 2 percent of accommodations cost more than $20,000.

The costs of litigation resulting from ADA also can be high. Since enforcement of the Act began in July 1992, it quickly has become a major component of employment law—one to which employers increasingly have had to respond. Through the end of fiscal year 1998, 108,939 ADA charges had been filed with EEOC, and 106,988 of those charges had been resolved. Of the resolved charges, 86 percent were either dropped or investigated and dismissed by EEOC but not without imposing opportunity costs and legal fees on employers. The other 14 percent of the charges led to a finding of discrimination by EEOC or a private settlement at an average cost to employers of $14,325 (not including opportunity costs and legal fees).

Although employers can be and are sued for discriminatory hiring, most litigation under ADA arises when employees are fired. The two most common violations of ADA alleged in charges filed with EEOC have involved, first, discharge, layoff, or suspension and, second, failure to provide reasonable accommodation. Thus, firms may have responded to the prospect of litigation by reducing their hiring of the disabled.

Has ADA Worked as Intended?

Although ADA may have caused employers to accommodate people with disabilities, the cost of complying with the Act may have reduced the demand for disabled workers and thereby have undone ADA's intended effects. To determine the employment effect of ADA, I analyzed data for a sample of men aged 18 to 65 from the Survey of Income and Program Participation (SIPP).

Table 1 compares changes in the employment rates of disabled and nondisabled men before and after enactment of ADA. Employment of men with disabilities fell by 10.9 percentage points following the enactment of ADA, while employment of nondisabled men fell by 3.1 percentage points. Thus, ADA re-

Table 1. Effect of ADA on Employment of Men with Disabilities

	Employment rate (percent) and change in employment rate (percentage points)	
	Men with disabilities	Men without disabilities
Before enactment of ADA (1985–1990)	59.8	95.5
After enactment of ADA (1991–April 1995)	48.9	92.4
Change in employment rate	–10.9*	–3.1*
Employment effect of ADA	**–7.8***	

*Change is significantly different from 0 at a 95-percent confidence level.

Survey of Income and Program Participation (SIPP).

duced the employment of disabled men by 7.8 percentage points.

Has ADA reduced employment of disabled workers of all types or have ADA's negative effects been concentrated in a few demographic categories? Using the sample of working-age men from the SIPP data, I estimated the effects of ADA on employment rates for disabled men according to their level of education, type of disability, and age (specified by decade of birth). I controlled for such other factors as occupation, industry, minority status, length of disability, and whether a disability resulted from an injury. . . . Relative employment fell in all cases, and all but 2 of the 24 estimates are statistically significant at the 95-percent confidence level.

To summarize:

• ADA caused a decrease of about 8 percentage points in the employment rate of men with disabilities.

• ADA caused lower employment regardless of age, educational level, and type of disability.

• Those most affected by ADA were young, less-educated and mentally disabled men.

ADA is a striking example of the law of unintended consequences. ADA has reduced employment opportunities not only for disabled people as a whole but especially for the most vulnerable groups—the young (less experienced), less educated (less skilled), and mentally disabled—groups that find it most difficult to get jobs.

Why has ADA had these consequences? Firms generally have reduced their employment of the disabled because the Act has imposed higher accommodation costs than firms would voluntarily incur. The burden of cost has fallen especially hard on those workers least likely to have been accommodated voluntarily by firms in the absence of ADA, namely, less-experienced and less-skilled workers and workers with mental disabilities, which generally are more difficult to accommodate than physical disabilities.

Findings of Other Research

The results in Table 1 are consistent with other studies. . . . For example, in a 1997 study, I used data from the Panel Study of Income Dynamics to estimate employment regressions similar to those estimated using the SIPP data.

A 1998 study by Daron Acemoglu and Joshua Angrist confirmed those results by using data from a different source. Acemoglu and Angrist noted that, in principle, the antidiscrimination mandate of ADA that allows disabled workers to sue their employers for wrongful termination could increase the employment of disabled workers by reducing turnover. Acemoglu and Angrist argued, however, that such "firing costs" are more likely to have caused a reduction in the hiring of disabled workers, an argument confirmed by their empirical analysis of data from the Current Population Survey. They found that ADA caused a large drop in the number of weeks worked by disabled men but no drop in the number of weeks worked by nondisabled men; the drop in weeks worked by disabled men appeared to result from less hiring of disabled workers.

Acemoglu and Angrist also separately examined the effects of ADA on firms of small, medium, and large size. They found the largest drop in weeks worked was at firms of medium size. That finding is consistent with the conclusion that ADA reduces the employment of disabled workers because firms with fewer than 15 employees are exempt from ADA regulations and large firms are better equipped than medium-size firms to accommodate disabled workers.

What Should We Do?

Substantial barriers to the employment of people with disabilities persist in spite of the employment mandates of ADA. In fact, the threat of litigation and ADA's accommodation mandate may even raise the barrier for many disabled workers by raising the cost of hiring them.

What policies would better assist the disabled? If the cost of the accommodation mandate has led employers to reduce their employment of the disabled, should the nondiscrimination mandate be enforced more rigorously so as to raise the cost of noncompliance? Or is there a need for a new strategy for increasing the employment of disabled Americans?

One new strategy that holds promise is to create a Disabled Workers Tax Credit (DWTC)—modeled on the Earned Income Tax Credit (EITC)—as proposed by Richard Burkhauser, Andrew Glenn, and D.C. Wittenburg. DWTC would provide a wage subsidy for disabled workers to encourage them to remain in or reenter the workplace after becoming disabled. The wage subsidy, even if given directly to workers, effectively would reduce the cost of hiring and accommodating them. That, in turn, would increase the ability of firms to hire them.

Although DWTC is still being assessed, experience with EITC suggests that DWTC could work. Empirical studies have found EITC to be successful at increasing labor force participation and reducing poverty among poor families.

Although a DWTC-like program would be yet another government program, it is likely to be both cheaper and more effective than forcing the hiring of disabled workers through the employment mandates of ADA.

Additional Civil Rights Protection for Gays and Lesbians Would Be Harmful

by Mathew D. Staver

About the author: *Mathew D. Staver is president and general counsel for the Liberty Counsel, a conservative civil liberties education and legal defense organization dedicated to preserving religious freedom.*

The federal Civil Rights Act of 1964 laid the foundation for future civil rights laws. The two driving forces behind the Civil Rights Act of 1964 arose primarily out of discrimination against African-Americans and women. Homosexual activists are attempting to hijack the civil rights train by claiming that homosexual behavior deserves the same special protection granted to racial and gender minorities. However, other than mimicking the rhetoric, the sexual preference movement has nothing in common with the civil rights movement.

Prior to the passage of the Civil Rights Act of 1964, the states ratified the Thirteenth, Fourteenth and Fifteenth Amendments, which were designed to abolish slavery and involuntary servitude, to afford the right of citizenship to any person born or naturalized in the United States, to guarantee that no person would be deprived of life, liberty or property without due process of law, to guarantee the equal protection of the laws, and to prevent the government from denying any person the right to vote on account of race, color or previous condition of servitude.

Despite the passage of these three constitutional amendments, discrimination against people of color continued. For many years, the country operated under the so-called "separate but equal" doctrine, which was not overturned until 1954. Paralleling the struggle of African-Americans and other people of color for civil rights was the women's suffrage movement. Women were not able to vote until 1920, when the Nineteenth Amendment was added to the United States Constitution. Despite these four constitutional amendments, widespread discrimination continued against women and people of color. The Civil Rights Act of 1964 was an attempt to remedy the ongoing discrimination.

Three Unifying Characteristics Are Required

The unifying characteristics of the protected classes within the Civil Rights Act of 1964 include (1) a history of longstanding, widespread discrimination, (2) economic disadvantage, and (3) immutable characteristics. The longstanding discrimination resulted in obvious economic disadvantage. Race, color, sex and national origin all share the same common bond of having immutable characteristics. Although religion is the sole category within the Civil Rights Act of 1964 that does not share the exact pattern of the immutable physical characteristics, the

> *"Elevating 'sexual orientation' to a protected civil right is economically, politically and socially divisive."*

characteristic of immutability or inalienability is deeply rooted in the founding of the country and became part of the First Amendment to the United States Constitution. All five categories within the Civil Rights Act of 1964 have specific constitutional amendments protecting each class. These constitutional amendments existed prior to the historic 1964 legislation.

"Sexual orientation" does not meet any of the three objective criteria shared by the historically protected civil rights categories. Thus, "sexual orientation" should not be elevated to the category of a protected civil right. At a recent public hearing in Orlando, Florida where the public was invited to speak about a proposal to add "sexual orientation" to the city code, the homosexual community could only find three people who presented potentially legitimate claims of employment discrimination. The rest of the comments focused on the desire to amend the code or hearsay of someone who faced discrimination twenty years ago! No one presented any information about discrimination in public facilities or housing. During the congressional debates over the Civil Rights Act of 1964 (which now fills almost 9,000 pages of *Congressional Record*), the stories of real discrimination were not hard to find.

The Homosexual Community Is Well Off

Typically real discrimination results in economic disadvantage. This is so because people are excluded from the political and economic marketplace. However, a person's "sexual orientation", or more accurately stated, "sexual preference", has not resulted in economic disadvantage. To the contrary, the homosexual community maintains an economic advantage over the heterosexual community. In 1991, the *Wall Street Journal* published information from the

Simmons Market Research Bureau and the United States Census data based on figures from 1988. The survey showed that the average annual income for homosexuals was over $55,430 compared to the national average of $32,144. Simmons Market Research Bureau's first survey was released in 1989. Their second survey, which was released in 1996, produced similar findings. The 1996 study found that 28% of gays earned more than $50,000, while 21% of gay households had incomes over $100,000. A gay research group known as Overlooked Opinions reported similar findings following a survey released in 1993. One internet census reported that 22% of gays and 20% of lesbians had an income of between $70,000 and $100,000, while 29% of gays and 16% of lesbians had incomes in excess of $100,000. This survey was based upon 2001 statistics of 6,351 individuals who identified themselves as gay, lesbian or transgender.

"Sexual orientation" does not include immutable characteristics. One need not debate whether homosexuality is genetic or social. The definition of "sexual orientation" includes the status of being, or the *perception* of being heterosexual, homosexual or bisexual. The definition therefore includes the entire spectrum of human sexuality. The lack of immutable characteristics creates a moving target, one that can change from day to day. The lack of immutable characteristics warns against elevating "sexual orientation" to a protected civil rights category.

Elevating "sexual orientation" to a protected civil right is economically, politically and socially divisive. History shows that the addition of "sexual orientation" to an anti-discrimination code results in frivolous lawsuits,

"Once homosexual, bisexual and transgender behavior is elevated to a protected status, there is nothing to stop . . . any other deviate sexual practice from receiving . . . protection."

which will wreak economic havoc upon the business community. Relying on a "sexual orientation" law in Tampa, Florida, a man dressed as a woman who worked for a company delivering sandwiches, claimed he was wrongfully terminated. The manager of the company received complaints from a hotel manager that the sandwich company employee was soliciting oral sex from military men who were guests at the hotel. The hotel manager told the sandwich company that it would no longer allow the delivery of sandwiches. When the sandwich company fired the employee, the employee filed a "sexual orientation" discrimination complaint.

According Special Status Will Result in Affirmative Action

Adding "sexual orientation" to a protected category causes political division. A number of cities throughout the country have repealed "sexual orientation" policies after they have been enacted. Political division is evident in Florida, where the homosexual community has become downright vicious where they now claim that local citizens committed fraud in obtain[ing] over 51,000 signatures (only 35,000 are required) for a referendum to repeal the "sexual orientation" ordinance.

According sexual preference special status will also create social division, resulting in a type of "affirmative action" for homosexual behavior. To implement Vermont's statewide "sexual orientation" law, Vermont issued a grant to an organization called Outright Vermont. The private organization used the state funds to teach about homosexual practices in the public schools. In addition to providing what the organization called "safer sex parties" in which students were given condoms, packages of lube, dental dams, and latex gloves and asked to demonstrate and practice "condom use", the organization also conducted a hormone needle use instructional program to educate participants regarding the proper use of needles to inject hormones for the purpose of altering gender characteristics.

In Milwaukee, Wisconsin, the public schools implemented the statewide "sexual orientation" law by training teachers and students about homosexual practices. A so-called heterosexual questionnaire asks the following question: "If you've never slept with a person of the same sex, is it possible that all you need is a good gay lover?" Including "sexual orientation" is merely the beginning rather than the end of the conflict. Future attempts will be made to add domestic partnerships, civil unions, and in some states there have been efforts to pursue same-sex marriage.

History and reason illustrate the insanity of according special civil rights protection to a person's sexual preference. Once homosexual, bisexual and transgender behavior is elevated to a protected status, there is nothing to stop bigamy, pedophilia, or any other deviate sexual practice from receiving the same protection. It should be remembered that when elevating any activity to special status, opposing activities and viewpoints lose protection. If "sexual orientation" laws become commonplace, then any person who speaks against deviant sexual practices will be vilified, their rights will be thwarted, and their freedom of religion and of conscious will be crushed.

Increasing the Penalties for Housing Discrimination Will Harm Society

by George C. Leef

About the author: *George C. Leef is an adjunct professor of law and economics at Northwood University, and a scholar with the Mackinac Center for Public Policy.*

Not so long ago in this country, you could stay out of legal trouble by refraining from aggression against other people. The law of torts, crimes, and property was well established and under those bodies of law, you committed no offense unless you acted so as to hurt another by taking or damaging something that was rightfully his. If you declined an offer to deal with someone else, you were perfectly within your rights because you had committed no aggression. Just saying "No" would cause you no legal difficulty.

That is no longer the case. With the passage of a host of federal and state antidiscrimination laws, individuals can now find themselves subject to suit and compelled to pay staggering legal fees and damage awards because they had the temerity to say "No" to someone in a "protected class." Some of the most egregious instances of the use of the law to punish people for making peaceful decisions regarding their own property have occurred in the rental-housing market. A recent decision by the Michigan Supreme Court highlights the continuing attack on the rights of property owners.

John and Terry Hoffius own an apartment building in Jackson, Michigan. In the summer of 1993, they had a vacancy and advertised it. They were contacted by a couple, Kristal McCready and Keith Kerr, who expressed interest in renting it. When asked if they were married, McCready and Kerr replied in the negative. Mr. Hoffius informed them that according to his religious beliefs it was sinful to cohabit out of wedlock and that he would not countenance it by renting to them.

McCready and Kerr soon found another apartment in the area but would not just let the matter drop. They contacted the Jackson County Fair Housing Center for assistance and then filed suit in state court against the Hoffiuses.

The case ran into a snag in the trial court, however. The judge was persuaded that in passing the Civil Rights Act (CRA), the state legislature did not mean to include unmarried couples in the class of people "protected" by the law. The reason was that an old Michigan statute made unmarried cohabitation a misdemeanor. Reasoning that the legislature would have repealed that statute if it had meant to "protect" unmarried couples against housing discrimination, the trial court dismissed the complaint. The plaintiffs appealed, but the state court of appeals affirmed the decision of the trial court.

The Unmarried Couple's Civil Rights Were Violated

But the plaintiffs had one more chance, the Michigan Supreme Court. They hit the jackpot. In a 4-2 decision, the Supreme Court reversed the decision of the court of appeals and held that it was a violation of the plaintiffs' "rights" under the CRA to refuse them an apartment because they were unmarried. The majority's arguments and rhetoric bear close scrutiny.

First, the court brushed off the argument that had persuaded the lower courts, namely the evident conflict between the anti-cohabitation statute and the CRA. Why, that statute hadn't been enforced in decades, said the court, and therefore it was going to presume that the legislature did mean to include unmarried couples under the CRA.

> *"Since everyone can obtain housing through the . . . free market, there is no 'state interest' . . . in trying to force open every housing door to every person."*

Second, and getting to the heart of the matter, the court declared that the Hoffiuses' property rights and religious convictions were of much less importance in its political-judicial view of the world than the "need" to provide "equal access" to housing and to "eradicate" discrimination. Enter one of the most pernicious phrases ever to find its way into the language: "compelling state interest."

According to the court, housing is a "fundamental need" and therefore the state has a "compelling interest" in ensuring that "no one be denied equal access to housing." And having uttered the magic phrase "compelling state interest," the court then was able to conclude that whatever rights the Hoffiuses might have are "outweighed" by the great need for government intervention in their decision-making.

A Free Market Guarantees Equal Access to All

It is hard to see how an abstraction, the state, can have any interests at all, but let's play along with the word game and assume that it does. Why is there a "compelling" interest in making sure that everyone has "equal access" to housing? In one sense, people have always had equal access so long as the law did not keep anyone from trying to contract with another for housing. McCready and Kerr were free to ask to rent an apartment from the Hoffiuses, and when they were turned down, they were free to go to other landlords with vacant apartments, which they did; and they quickly found comparable quarters. (If the Michigan law against cohabitation interfered with "equal access" to housing, then the solution would be to repeal it rather than to interfere with the liberty and property rights of the Hoffiuses.)

> *"Laws against housing discrimination have no place in a free society."*

In a free market, everyone with the means to purchase housing (or food, cars, clothing, and everything else) is able to get the goods and services he needs. The great majority of landlords are interested only in the ability of the prospective tenant to pay the rent and take reasonably good care of the property. Most care no more about the marital status of their tenants than they care about their ice-cream preferences. A small number, however, do care about what the law has deemed to be "forbidden grounds" (to borrow the title of Professor Richard Epstein's book), but their preferences—their "discrimination"—is easily bypassed. Long before there were any anti-discrimination statutes, people who were generally unpopular learned to go where they were welcome and avoid places where they were not.

The market provides housing for all, and the fact that a few landlords have what politicians and judges call irrational preferences is no justification for the use of coercion against them. Since everyone can obtain housing through the peaceful processes of the free market, there is no "state interest" at all in trying to force open every housing door to every person.

One of the arguments raised by counsel for the Hoffiuses was that there was no need to trample upon his clients' freedom because there are less obtrusive means of ensuring that people can find housing than to force landlords to rent to people whose conduct they find offensive. But the court also brushed that aside, saying, "We have not identified a less obtrusive alternative to eradicate discrimination in real estate transactions."

Anti-Discrimination Laws Force Political Correctness

Most revealing. Obviously aware that there are noncoercive means of helping people find housing if they can't find it on their own, the court says that there is no other way of "eradicating discrimination" than by lawsuits and mandates. The real reason for housing discrimination laws is thus revealed—molding landlords into a politically correct image of perfect indifference to the habits and characteristics of the people who live in their buildings. At one point, the court suggests that if the Hoffiuses don't like the restrictions on their freedom, they can just get out of the rental-housing business. That, I suggest, is the real agenda of the "housing activists." They want to make life so miserable for people of conviction that eventually all landlords will be meek, compliant order-takers.

This case is far from unique. There have been suits over this precise issue in several other states, notably California and Massachusetts, with the plaintiffs winning. Mr. Hoffius may appeal to the United States Supreme Court, arguing that the First Amendment should shield him from the state's interference with his right to select his own tenants. While I would hope he would win on that ground, in truth this case is not about religious freedom. It is about property rights. Because he owns the building, he should be free to say yes or no to prospective tenants for any reason whatsoever. The Constitution was meant to protect the rights of property owners to manage their affairs free from governmental confiscation or interference just as much as it was meant to protect the First Amendment freedoms. Landlords who do not want to rent to unmarried couples for religious reasons should not be treated any differently than, say, landlords who do not want to rent to families with children for noise reasons.

If the housing activists are really concerned about the prospect of individuals' not being able to find housing because of discrimination, they can solve the supposed problem by purchasing or constructing rental-housing units and offering them on a pristinely nondiscriminatory basis. They could even eliminate the most pervasive kind of discrimination of all—discrimination against people who want to live in a certain place but can't afford the rent—by charging little or no rent at all. No law prevents housing activists from using their own resources to solve the "problem" of discrimination.

But of course, we will never see that. It is easier and far less costly for the activists to enter the political arena and work for coercive statutes that make other people bear the costs for what they want than to try to solve the problem themselves. What we really need to eradicate in America is not "discrimination" but rather the notion that it is all right to use coercion against others to get what you want.

The Hoffius case will now go back to trial on the issue of damages. The plaintiffs are claiming that they suffered "emotional distress" as a result of being turned down. How much a jury might choose to award is anyone's guess. A sensible jury would say that the plaintiffs haven't really suffered any damage at all and award nothing, but it is more likely that it will be swayed by lawyerly "Send them a message!" rhetoric that has in other discrimination cases led to damage awards in the millions. Furthermore, Mr. Hoffius will almost certainly be ordered to pay the plaintiffs' attorney fees, now in excess of $30,000. He may be financially ruined just because he said "No" to the wrong people.

Laws against housing discrimination have no place in a free society. They solve an imaginary problem with a vicious and wasteful means that hastens the erosion of freedom.

The Fight for African American Slavery Reparations Impedes the Advancement of Civil Rights

by Robert Tracinski

About the author: *Robert Tracinski is the editor of the* Intellectual Activist, *a magazine that champions the power of reason, the value of the individual, and the freedom of a capitalist society.*

Over the past few years, a movement composed of liability lawyers and self-titled "civil rights activists" has been trying to revive a deservedly obscure idea: the payment of reparations for the injustices committed under slavery. These activists are undeterred by the fact that none of the original victims or villains of slavery are still alive. Reparations, they say, should be paid by the US government and some long-lived corporations, to compensate the current-day descendants of slaves for the wrongs done to their ancestors.

The most prominent step toward reparations is the formation, late [in 2000], of the Reparations Assessment Group, a consortium of academics and liability lawyers led by Harvard Law School Professor Charles Ogletree. The group was formed to prepare civil lawsuits against the federal government and some corporations, ostensibly on behalf of the descendants of slaves.

The case for such reparations is two-fold. First, reparations activists claim that compensation to the descendants of slaves is just, because today's blacks are the "victims" of slavery, and "the victims of unjust enrichment should be compensated." Second, they claim that reparations would help "bridge the racial divide" in America and "heal the wounds of slavery."

In reality, reparations would be a gross injustice, punishing innocent people for a crime they did not commit. Even worse, the campaign for reparations will not "heal the wounds of slavery" but will perpetuate racial conflict.

In order to understand why the campaign for reparations is unjust, we have to look, not just at legal precedent, but at the basic moral principles at the foundation of American law.

One of those principles is the idea that justice is *individual*, not racial. Human beings exist as individuals, with each person responsible for his own choices and actions and entitled to be judged on his own character, not on the color of his skin. By contrast, racism consists of treating a person, not as a self-responsible individual, but as an interchangeable cog of some larger racial collective.

If this racist view is implemented in law, the result is manifestly unjust. Suppose, for example, that a bank robber has just made his getaway, and the police are in hot pursuit. All they know about the criminal is that witnesses say he was black. So they round up the first black man they find, haul him off to jail, give him a summary trial, and send him to prison for life. He protests that he is not the person who robbed the bank, but his tormenters say: "Who cares? We know that this crime was committed by a black person, and we punished a black person. It doesn't matter which one."

If this example does not sound entirely fictional, it certainly is not. This was the racist approach behind lynchings in the Old South.

Individual Justice vs. Racism

The premise behind every form of racism, we must bear in mind, is the rejection of the principle that justice is individual. As the novelist and philosopher Ayn Rand observed, "Racism is the lowest, most crudely primitive form of collectivism. . . . [It] means, in practice, that a man is to be judged, not by his own character and actions, but by the characters and actions of a collective of ancestors." The racist approach consists of declaring that an individual's own thoughts and choices are irrelevant; all that matters, to the racist, is a person's membership in a racial group.

Racism, as a philosophical and legal issue, comes down to one basic question: Is justice collective, i.e., should a person be judged by his race—or is justice individual, i.e., should a person be judged on his own merits.

By this standard, how do reparations for slavery measure up?

Let us examine the attempt to seek reparations through the tort laws. The purpose of tort law is to provide compensation to persons who have been unjustly harmed, to be paid by those persons who are responsible for the harm. To have a legitimate case for reparations, one must first identify an individual who has been directly, provably harmed—and then one must identify an individual who is directly, provably responsible for that harm.

Yet that is precisely what *cannot* be done in this case. Every individual slave and every individual slaveholder is long dead. There is no person living who can be a party to a lawsuit seeking reparations for slavery—*and* there is no individual still alive who can be brought before the court and named as the defendant.

This, incidentally, is a crucial difference between reparations for slavery and reparations for Japanese-Americans who were interned during World War II, or Jews whose assets were stolen during the Holocaust. In both of those cases, victims of the injustice were still alive and able to seek compensation, although in some cases compensation for stolen wealth was also awarded to the direct, first-generation descendants of victims who had died.

The case of slavery, however, is fundamentally different. It is an attempt to extend liability, not merely one generation, but through multiple generations, into the *indefinite* past.

The Victims of Slavery Are Dead

The absurdity of this attempt is captured in a single sentence from a news report on this issue, which describes "a growing number of slave descendants who are calling for the US government to repay them for 246 years of bondage." The absurdity is that these people cannot be "re-paid" for 246 years of bondage, because they did not experience that bondage. The people who are demanding reparations have never been slaves. Moreover, their parents were not slaves, and, except in a few extraordinary cases, their grandparents were not slaves. In a normal case, we have to look back at least *four to five generations* to find ancestors who were actually slaves.

So those who are alive today, who are seeking reparations for slavery, are not in any way the direct victims of slavery. Their connection to the people who actually were slaves is long and remote, traced through more than a century of parents and grandparents who were free to make their own choices, guide their own actions, and pursue their own fortunes. This intervening history makes it impossible to determine objectively the degree or even the existence of slavery's effect on current-day descendants of slaves.

> "The campaign for reparations will not 'heal the wounds of slavery' but will perpetuate racial conflict."

As a parallel example, consider the tens of millions of Americans who are descended from immigrants who came to the country about a century ago. Many of these immigrants came to America with no money, no education, no specialized skills, and no knowledge of the English language. Many, such as Eastern European Jews, had been victims of persecution in their native lands. Yet most of these immigrants worked to pull themselves out of poverty, their children were able to rise into the middle class, their grandchildren attended college—and today, we do not talk about the "lingering legacy of immigration," nor do descendants of immigrants seek reparations for the past persecution of their ancestors. After three or four generations, it is clear that the choices and actions of individuals have had a far greater impact on their well-being than the past condition of their ancestors.

It is important to recognize that the history of blacks in America is not fundamentally different. In the century after slavery—despite legal segregation and the continued influence of racism—black Americans improved their own condition by every measure. Labor force participation rates for blacks were usually higher than for whites, and as a result black poverty rates dropped consistently over the entire century. Other economic and cultural ills were largely absent within a few decades after slavery's end: Black crime rates were no higher than for other groups, and illegitimacy rates were well below 20%. The work and effort of former slaves and their immediate descendants in the century after 1865 largely overcame the injuries suffered by their ancestors.

> *"History shows the absurdity of the claim that people living today are entitled to compensation for injuries suffered by their ancestors in the indefinite past."*

Expansion of the Welfare State

Incidentally, this gives the lie to the claim that poverty, unemployment, crime, and illegitimacy are the "legacy of slavery." Every one of these ills became epidemic only *after 1960*. It was after the creation of the "Great Society" welfare programs, with their perverse incentives against work and marriage, and the passage of the Civil Rights Act of 1964, which laid the legal foundation for racial preferences, that black crime and illegitimacy rates soared, labor force participation dropped, and poverty rates froze. It is significant that reparations advocates, almost without exception, seek to *expand* the welfare state. In blaming slavery for every problem faced by black Americans, they are trying to divert attention from the disastrous legacy of welfare and "affirmative action."

This history shows the absurdity of the claim that people living today are entitled to compensation for injuries suffered by their ancestors in the indefinite past. Instead, it shows that individuals are capable of taking responsibility for improving their own lives—and indeed, that they fail to progress only when they are convinced *not* to accept that responsibility.

So much for the plaintiff's side of the equation. What about the defendant? Is there anyone alive today who may legitimately be punished for the injustices of slavery? How, for example, can a white American today be fined for an injustice that might have been committed by his great-great-grandfather?

The problem is compounded by the fact that the majority of Americans do not descend from slaveholders; their ancestors were either from the non-slaveholding North, or they were immigrants who came to America after the end of slavery. But even if we can find someone of pure slaveholding stock, as it were, someone whose ancestors were all guilty of the crime of slavery—how can we hold that person, today, responsible for actions taken more than a century ago by his forebears? To do so, we would have to judge this person—to quote Ayn Rand, "not by his own character and actions, but by the characters and actions of a collective of ancestors." Yet that is the very essence of racism.

Reparations advocates have offered no answer—literally none—to this argument. The response of Representative John Conyers, who has been promoting reparations in Congress, is typical: "This is not a blame game. We are not looking for who did it or how evil were their motives. Payment is not going to come from who did it. The government assumes responsibility." In other words, Conyers attempts to evade the issue by pretending that "the government"—and not the individuals who pay taxes—will foot the bill.

Are Government and Corporations Responsible?

In that spirit, the proposed reparations suits would target two kinds of legal entities that *are* still "alive" from the days of slavery: the government and those corporations that have been in continuous existence since before 1865. Remember that reparations advocates still have not identified someone with standing to sue, so there is still no proper plaintiff. But they argue that we do have a defendant, that the federal government and private corporations can be held culpable for the evils of slavery.

Let us consider the federal government first.

Seeking compensation from the United States government evades the fact that the federal government has already paid an enormous cost to *end* slavery by fighting the Civil War. Even if we do not count the cost in human lives, which was enormous, we can at least count the cost in dollars. The Civil War cost the US government about $15 billion—an astronomical sum in 1865, equivalent to hundreds of billions of dollars today. Adding 135 years of compound interest—a typical technique used to calculate demands for reparations—the federal government's cost rises to trillions of dollars in current value.

More fundamentally, however, the federal government has no funds of its own, no cache of savings left over from, say, taxes on cotton. All of the government's money is extracted from today's taxpayers. The government is merely a middleman who would pass the cost for reparations on to the taxpayers. That leaves us where we began: the manifest injustice of punishing people for the crimes committed by some of their distant ancestors.

> *"Rather than healing historical wounds, [a racial concept of justice] is an approach guaranteed to keep those wounds open forever."*

Now let us turn to the second proposed defendant: corporations.

The proposed reparations suits would target a few long-lived corporations which at one time used slave labor or profited indirectly from slavery. On this basis, the proposed suits would lay claim to some significant portion of the current assets of these corporations. Early [in 2001], for example, the state of California passed a law requiring every insurance company that does business in California—which includes every major American insurance company—to disclose whether it once offered "slave insurance," insurance offered to protect slave-owners against financial losses from the death or escape of a slave. The law was clearly designed to aid in building a reparations case against these corporations.

The Case Cannot Be Proven

Such lawsuits, however, face a fundamental barrier: How would one prove that the current assets or profits of a corporation are caused by profits made more than 135 years ago under slavery? Consider the following example.

The first major insurance company to comply with the California law was Aetna, which has been in existence since the 1840s. A search of Aetna's records revealed a total of *five* slave insurance policies. That is a minuscule amount for a major insurance company. But also reflect on what has happened since. Aetna, for example, was reorganized in the late 1860s,

> *"The motive of reparations advocates becomes clear. . . . They seek to use their group's past history of slavery as a license to enslave others."*

radically changed its practices to weather a series of economic depressions in the 1870s, and went on to survive through wars, through the Great Depression, and through every economic event that has occurred since.

It is obvious that after 135 years of ups and downs, during which time fortunes have risen and fallen, thousands of new companies have been formed, thousands of old ones have gone out of existence, and the nation's economy has been radically transformed twice, first by heavy industry, then by information technology—after all of this time, any profits once gained from slavery have been rendered irrelevant.

A tort claim that attempts to trace a portion of a company's profits from 135 years ago to its assets today is arbitrary and unreasonable. It is like the claim that the flapping of a butterfly's wings in the Amazon causes a hurricane in the Northern Atlantic. It is, in principle, unprovable.

More fundamentally, any such unlimited liability subjects the current stockholders of a company to the arbitrary and unpredictable expropriation of their wealth. If the current owners of an asset may be punished without limit for the wrongs committed by its past owners, then no one could ever hold clear title to a single piece of property or share of stock.

In all such cases, the principle of individual justice demands a statute of limitations. As a precedent, consider the common practice of corporations making 99-year contracts, signing 99-year leases, issuing 99-year bonds. This common-law custom means that, although a corporation may continue to exist for many centuries, no legal agreement can extend beyond a single century, because no one who was old enough to be legally responsible at the time the agreement was made will still be alive 99 years later. The underlying premise is that no legal agreement can be binding on future generations in perpetuity. There has to be limit, a cutoff beyond which new generations cannot be bound by the promises and agreements of their ancestors.

Liability Cannot Be Unlimited

The same truth applies to liability. There has to be a cutoff beyond which the current owners of corporations and estates cannot be held responsible, in perpetuity, for the deeds of their predecessors—including the crime of slavery.

There is only one approach under which such unlimited ancestral liability appears to make sense. The only way to extend past grievances indefinitely to future generations is to throw out any concern with punishing or compensating specific individuals. Reparations only makes sense if we focus, not on individuals, but on racial groups. Reparations require that we hold all whites today responsible for what other whites did 135 years ago—and that we compensate all blacks today for what happened to other blacks before 1865. To do this, we have to regard each individual as just an interchangeable cog in his racial group.

From an individualist perspective, there is neither a proper plaintiff nor a proper defendant in this suit. To reparations advocates, however, these parties are easy to identify—so long as one agrees to abandon individual justice and herd mankind into racial collectives. From this perspective of racial collectivism, the plaintiff in this case is "black America," which is seeking compensation from the defendant, "white America."

Some reparations advocates openly acknowledge this collectivist approach. Tulane University Professor Robert Westley notes that the demand for reparations is the result of a "sea-change . . . regarding the proper evaluation of the anti-racist agenda set by the Civil Rights Movement" which "relied on the rhetoric of equality rights." Westley goes on to say—correctly—that this "liberal legal framework" and its notion of equal rights is the primary barrier to reparations—which he says must be overcome. In a truly Orwellian[1] climax, he quotes the work of Professor Thomas Pettigrew, who defines "the new racism" to include "individualistic conceptions of how opportunity and social stratification operate in American society." In other words, individualism is racism. Westley attempts to wipe out the concept of individual justice, establishing racial collectivism as the only basis for morality and law.

Reparations Would Not Help Heal the Wounds of Slavery

This gives the lie to the claim that reparations will "heal the wounds" of slavery and racism. Reparations would do the opposite: they would promote a collectivist, racial concept of justice. The philosophical perspective behind repara-

---

1. A reference to author George Orwell's book *1984*, a social and political allegory in which individualism no longer exists.

tions encourages men to look on their fellows, not as individuals with their own independent characters and merits, but only as members of some competing, antagonistic racial collective.

Rather than healing historical wounds, this is an approach that is guaranteed to keep those wounds open forever.

For an example, look no farther than the current bloodbath in the Balkans. This conflict can be traced back to grievances more than 600 years old. The Field of the Blackbirds, for example, is a battlefield in Kosovo where a Serbian army was defeated by the Ottoman Turks in the year 1389. This sounds like ancient history to us—but not to the Serbs. For them, the Field of the Blackbirds represents their tribe's history of suffering and oppression.

To the Serbs, it does not matter that everyone who fought in the battle is long dead or that the political entities they fought for dissolved centuries ago. The Serbs cling to the memory of this battle because it is part of the history of their ethnic group. It does not matter which individuals were involved or whether they are still alive—because the racial collective, in this view, lives on. And in the name of this racial collective, the Serbs are still fighting the same battle against the same rival tribes.

The Field of the Blackbirds is an eloquent symbol of a certain kind of mentality, a way of thinking that is taking hold in America and threatens to plunge us into the same kind of ethnic warfare that is currently laying waste to the former Yugoslavia.

America's Field of the Blackbirds is slavery.

If you want to project the kind of racial conflict that slavery is being used to justify, consider the demands made by reparations advocates. What do they regard as adequate compensation for their ancestors' enslavement?

The bidding starts at $1.4 trillion. One organization asks for $6 trillion, enough to give $20,000 in cash to every single black American—though an activist who promotes this figure describes it as a bare minimum "pittance." Georgetown University Professor Richard America claims that reparations should be as high as $10 trillion. *Time* magazine columnist Jack White doubles the damages for pain and suffering, adds compound interest, and arrives at a figure of $24 trillion. Either as part of these reparations, or in addition to them, activists also demand such special favors as free college education for all American blacks.

Blacks Would Become the Favored Class

For reference, the gross domestic product of the United States—the total annual output of our entire economy—is about $8 trillion. It is obvious that meeting a demand for 10 to 24 trillion dollars in reparations would require massive, systematic expropriation of wealth from whites. Jack White, who suggested the $24 trillion figure, suggests that it be paid over a period of 250 years in the form of subsidies and special favors for blacks. The time frame is no coincidence. In effect, White seeks to redress slavery—250 years in which blacks were an oppressed class forced to provide unpaid labor—with 250 years in which blacks can be a *favored* class, living off the unpaid labor of others.

In this light, the motive of reparations advocates becomes clear. They do not seek a measured compensation for some specific, provable harm. They seek to use their group's past history of slavery as a license to enslave others.

Most advocates do not seem to believe that this goal can be achieved either through Congress or the courts. Perversely, that seems to be part of the attraction of the reparations movement. By making a claim to racial "justice" so outrageously unjust that it will never be granted by "white America," reparations advocates are deliberately setting an unachievable goal. The motive: As US Representative Bobby Rush threatens, "The future of race relations will be determined by reparations for slavery." The demand for reparations, if it is accepted by a majority of blacks, would disfigure American race relations with an un-salvable open sore—a perpetual, ineradicable basis for future racial grievance.

This is the manner in which the campaign for reparations is pushing America in the same direction as the former Yugoslavia. Reparation advocates claim that they want to achieve their aims in the courts, under the civilized cover of legal arguments and procedures. But they are promoting the same philosophy that sent the Serbs into the streets with guns—and that philosophy is every bit as dangerous to Americans, both black and white, as it was to the people of every ethnic background who used to coexist in Yugoslavia.

Chapter 3

Is Affirmative Action Beneficial?

Affirmative Action: An Overview

by *CQ Researcher*

About the author: CQ Researcher, *published by Congressional Quarterly, is a weekly publication that provides background information and analysis on timely topics.*

African-Americans and other racial and ethnic minority groups have been underrepresented on college campuses throughout U.S. history. The civil rights revolution has effectively dismantled most legal barriers to higher education for minorities. But the social and economic inequalities that persist between white Americans and racial and ethnic minority groups continue to make the goal of equal opportunity less than reality for many African-Americans and Hispanics.

The legal battles that ended mandatory racial segregation in the United States began with higher education nearly two decades before the Supreme Court's historic ruling in *Brown v. Board of Education.* In the first of the rulings that ended the doctrine of "separate but equal," the court in 1938 ruled that Missouri violated a black law school applicant's equal protection rights by offering to pay his tuition to an out-of-state school rather than admit him to the state's all-white law school.

The court followed with a pair of rulings in 1950 that similarly found states guilty of violating black students' rights to equal higher education. Texas was ordered to admit a black student to the state's all-white law school rather than force him to attend an inferior all-black school. And Oklahoma was found to have discriminated against a black student by admitting him to a previously all-white state university but denying him the opportunity to use all its facilities.

At the time of these decisions, whites had substantially greater educational opportunities than African-Americans. As of 1950, a majority of white Americans ages 25–29—56 percent—had completed high school, compared with only 24 percent of African-Americans. Eight percent of whites in that age group had completed college compared with fewer than 3 percent of blacks. Most of the

African-American college graduates had attended all-black institutions: either private colleges established for blacks or racially segregated state universities.

The Supreme Court's 1954 decision in *Brown* to begin dismantling racial segregation in elementary and secondary education started to reduce the inequality in educational opportunities for whites and blacks, but changes were slow. It was not until 1970 that a majority of African-Americans ages 25–29 had attained high school degrees.

Changes at the nation's elite colleges and universities were even slower. In their book *The Shape of the River*, two former Ivy League presidents—Bowen and Derek Bok—say that as of 1960 "no selective college or university was making determined efforts to seek out and admit substan-

> *"Many universities instituted 'affirmative action' programs that included . . . recruitment of minority applicants as well as explicit use of race . . . in admissions policies."*

tial numbers of African-American students." As of 1965, they report, African-Americans comprised only 4.8 percent of students on the nation's college campuses and fewer than 1 percent of students at select New England colleges.

As part of the Civil Rights Act of 1964, Congress included provisions in Title IV to authorize the Justice Department to initiate racial-desegregation lawsuits against public schools and colleges and to require the U.S. Office of Education (now the Department of Education) to give technical assistance to school systems undergoing desegregation. A year later, President Lyndon B. Johnson delivered his famous commencement speech at historically black Howard University that laid the foundation for a more proactive approach to equalizing opportunities for African-Americans. "You do not take a person," Johnson said, "who, for years, has been hobbled by chains and liberate him, bring him up to the starting line of a race and then say, 'You are free to compete with all the others,' and still justly believe that you have been completely fair."

Affirmative Action Targets Minorities

Colleges began in the mid-1960s to make deliberate efforts to increase the number of minority students. Many universities instituted "affirmative action" programs that included targeted recruitment of minority applicants as well as explicit use of race as a factor in admissions policies. White students challenged the use of racial preferences, but the Supreme Court—in the [*University of California Regents v.*] *Bakke* decision in 1978—gave colleges and universities a flashing green light to consider race as one factor in admissions policies aimed at ensuring a racially diverse student body.

The federal government encouraged universities to look to enrollment figures as the criterion for judging the success of their affirmative action policies. By requiring universities to report minority enrollment figures, the Nixon administration appeared to suggest that race-conscious admissions were "not only permissible but mandatory," according to Bowen and Bok. But universities were also motivated, they say, to remedy past racial discrimination, to educate minority leaders and to create diversity on campuses.

As early as 1966, Bowen and Bok report, Harvard Law School moved to increase the number of minority students by "admitting black applicants with test scores far below those of white classmates." As other law schools adopted the strategy, enrollment of African-Americans increased—from 1 percent of all law students in 1965 to 4.5 percent in 1975. Similar efforts produced a significant increase in black students in Ivy League colleges. The proportion of African-American students at Ivy League schools increased from 2.3 percent in 1967 to 6.7 percent in 1976, Bowen and Bok report.

Critics, predominantly but not exclusively political conservatives, charged that the racial preferences amounted to "reverse discrimination" against white students and applicants. Some white students challenged the policies in court. The Supreme Court sought to resolve the issue in 1978 in a case brought by a California man. Alan Bakke, who had been denied admission to the University of California Medical School at Davis under a system that explicitly reserved 16 of 100 seats for minority applicants. The 4-1-4 decision fell short of a definitive resolution, though.

Justice Lewis F. Powell Jr. cast the decisive vote in the case. He joined four justices to reject Davis' fixed-quota approach and four others to allow use of race as one factor in admissions decisions. In summarizing

> *"Critics . . . charged that the racial preferences amounted to 'reverse discrimination' against white students and applicants."*

his opinion from the bench, Powell explained that it meant Bakke would be admitted to the medical school but that Davis was free to adopt a more "flexible program designed to achieve diversity" just like those "proved to be successful at many of our great universities."

Civil rights advocates initially reacted with "consternation," according to [Sheldon] Steinbach, [general counsel] of the American Council on Education. Quickly, though, college officials and higher-education groups took up the invitation to devise programs that used race—in Powell's terms—as a "plus factor" without setting aside any seats specifically for minority applicants. The ruling, Steinbach says, "enabled institutions in a creative manner to legally provide for a diverse student body."

The Supreme Court has avoided re-examining *Bakke* since 1978, but has narrowed the scope of affirmative action in other areas. The court in 1986 ruled that government employers could not lay off senior white workers to make room for new minority hires, though it upheld affirmative action in hiring and promotions in two other decisions that year and another ruling in a sex-discrimination case a year later. As for government contracting, the court ruled in 1989 that state and local governments could not use racial preferences except to remedy past discrimination and extended that limitation to federal programs in 1995.

All of the court's decisions were closely divided, but the conservative majority made clear their discomfort with race-specific policies. Indeed, as legal-affairs writer Lincoln Caplan notes, none of the five current conservatives—Chief Justice William H. Rehnquist and Associate Justices Sandra Day O'Connor, Antonin Scalia, Anthony M. Kennedy and Clarence Thomas—has ever voted to approve a race-based affirmative action program.

Negative Reaction

A political and legal backlash against affirmative action emerged with full force in the 1990s—highlighted by moves in California to scrap race-conscious policies in the state's university system and a federal appeals court decision barring racial preferences in admissions in Texas and two neighboring states. But President Bill Clinton rebuffed calls to scrap federal affirmative action programs. And colleges continued to follow race-conscious admissions policies in the absence of a new Supreme Court pronouncement on the issue.

In the first of the moves against race-conscious admissions, the 5th U.S. Circuit Court of Appeals in New Orleans in March 1996 struck down the University of Texas Law School's system that used separate procedures for white and minority applicants with the goal of admitting a class with 5 percent African-American and 10 percent Mexican-American students. The ruling in the *Hopwood* [*v. Texas*] case unanimously rejected the university's attempt to justify the racial preferences on grounds of past discrimination. Two judges also rejected the university's diversity defense and directly contradicted the prevailing interpretation of *Bakke* that diversity amounted to a "compelling governmental interest" justifying race-based policies.

The ruling specifically applied only to the three states in the 5th Circuit—Louisiana, Mississippi and Texas—but observers saw the decision as significant. "This is incredibly big," said John C. Jeffries Jr., a University of Virginia law professor and Justice Powell's biographer. "This could affect every public institution in America because all of them take racial diversity in admissions."

Four months later, the University of California Board of Regents—policy-making body for the prestigious, 162,000-student state university system —narrowly voted to abolish racial and sexual preferences in admissions by fall 1997. The 14-10 vote approved a resolution submitted by a black businessman, Ward Connerly, and supported by the state's Republican governor, Pete Wilson. Connerly was also the driving force behind a voter initiative—Proposition 209—to abolish racial preferences in state government employment and contracting as well as college and university admissions. Voters approved the measure, 54 percent to 46 percent, in November 1996.

In the face of opposition from UC President Richard Atkinson, the move to scrap racial preferences was delayed to admissions for the 1998–1999 academic year. In May 1998, the university released figures showing a modest overall decline in acceptance by non-Asian minorities to 15.2 percent for the coming year from 17.6 percent for the 1997–1998 school year. But the figures also showed a steep drop in the number of black and Hispanic students in the entering classes at the two most prestigious campuses—Berkeley and UCLA. At Berkeley, African-American and Hispanic acceptances fell to 10.5 percent from 21.9 percent for the previous year; at UCLA, the drop was to 14.1 percent from 21.8 percent.

The Supreme Court did nothing to counteract the legal shift away from racial preferences in education. It declined in 1995 to review a decision by the federal appeals court in Richmond, Va., that struck down a University of Maryland scholarship program reserved for African-American students. A year later, the justices refused to hear Texas' appeal of the *Hopwood* decision; and a year after that they also turned aside a challenge by labor and civil rights groups to Proposition 209. Instead, the high court concentrated on a series of rulings beginning in June 1993 that limited the use of race in congressional and legislative redistricting. And in June 1995 the court issued a decision, *Adarand Constructors, Inc. v. Peña*, that limited the federal government's discretion to give minority-owned firms preferences in government contracting.

> *"Diversity in enrollment has 'far-reaching and significant benefits for all students, non-minorities and minorities alike.'"*

With affirmative action under sharp attack, Bowen and Bok came out in 1998 with their book-length study of graduates of selective colleges that they said refused many of the criticisms of race-based admissions. Using a database of some 80,000 students who entered 28 elite colleges and universities in 1951, 1976 and 1989, the two former Ivy League presidents confirmed the increase in minority enrollment at the schools and the impact of racial preferences: More than half the black students admitted in 1976 and 1989 would not have been admitted under race-neutral policies, they said. But they said dropout rates among black students were low, satisfaction with their college experiences high and post-graduation accomplishments comparable with—or better than—white graduates.

The Bowen-Bok book buttressed college and university officials in resisting calls to scrap racial preferences. While voters in Washington state moved to eliminate race-based admissions with an anti-affirmative action initiative in 1998, no other state university system followed the UC lead in voluntarily abolishing the use of race in weighing applications.

In Texas, then-Gov. George W. Bush sought to bolster minority enrollment in the UT system after *Hopwood* by proposing the 10 percent plan—guaranteeing admission to any graduating senior in the top 10 percent of his class. (Florida Gov. Jeb Bush followed suit with his 20 percent plan two years later.) Many schools—both public and private—re-examined their admissions policies after

Hopwood. But, according to Steinbach, most of them "found that what they had was satisfactory."

Legal Battles

Critics of race-based admissions kept up their pressure on the issue by waging expensive, protracted legal battles in four states: Georgia, Michigan, Texas and Washington. The cases produced conflicting decisions. The conflict was starkest in the two University of Michigan cases, where two judges both appointed in the 1980s by President Ronald Reagan reached different results in evaluating the use of race at the undergraduate college and at the law school.

The controversy in Michigan began in a sense with the discontent of a longtime Ann Arbor faculty member, Carl Cohen. A professor of philosophy and a "proud" member of the American Civil Liberties Union (ACLU), Cohen had been troubled by racial preferences since the 1970s. In 1995 he read a journal article that described admissions rates for black college applicants as higher nationally than those for white applicants. The article prompted Cohen to begin poking around to learn about Michigan's system.

As Cohen tells the story, administrators stonewalled him until he used the state's freedom of information law to obtain the pertinent documents. He found that the admissions offices used a grid system that charted applicants based on high school grade point average on a horizontal axis and standardized test scores on a vertical axis—and that there were separate grids or different "action codes" (reject or admit) for white applicants and for minority applicants. "The racially discriminatory policies of the university are blatant," Cohen says today. "They are written in black and white by the university. It's just incredible."

> *"The National Association of Scholars . . . found 'no connection . . . between campus racial diversity and the supposed educational benefits.'"*

Cohen wrote up his findings in a report that he presented later in the year at a meeting of the state chapter of the American Association of University Professors. The report also found its way to a Republican state legislator, Rep. Deborah Whyman, who conducted a hearing on the issue and later held a news conference to solicit unsuccessful applicants to challenge the university's admission system. They forwarded about 100 of the replies to the Center for Individual Rights, a conservative public-interest law firm already active in challenging racial preferences.

[Jennifer] Gratz and a second unsuccessful white applicant—Patrick Hamacher—were chosen to be the named plaintiffs in a class-action suit filed in federal court in Detroit in October 1997. The center filed a second suit against the law school's admission system in December 1997. The lead plaintiff was Barbara Grutter, who applied to the law school in December 1996 while in her 40s after raising a family and working as a health-care consultant. Grutter, who is white, thought she deserved admission based on her 3.8 undergraduate grade-point average 18 years earlier and a respectable score on the law school admission test (161, or 86th percentile nationally). Since the rejection, she has not enrolled elsewhere.

The cases proved to be long and expensive. By last fall [2000], the university said it had spent $4.3 million defending the two suits, not counting personnel costs; the center had spent $400,000, including salaries, and also received the equivalent of $1 million in pro bono legal services from a Minneapolis firm helping to litigate the suits. Among the key pieces of evidence was a long report by an Ann Arbor faculty member—psychology Professor Patricia Gurin—concluding that diversity in enrollment has "far-reaching and significant benefits for all students, non-minorities and minorities alike." The center countered with a lengthy study issued under the auspices of the National Association of Scholars that analyzed the same data and found "no connection . . . between campus racial diversity and the supposed educational benefits."

In the meantime, the university revised its undergraduate admissions system, beginning with the entering class of 1999. The race-based grids and codes were replaced by a numerical system that assigned points to each applicant based on any of a number of characteristics. An applicant from an "underrepresented minority group"—African-Americans, Hispanics and Native Americans—is given 20 points. (One hundred points is typically required for admission, according to Cohen.) The same number is given to an applicant from a disadvantaged socioeconomic status, to a white student from a predominantly minority high school or to a scholarship athlete, according to university counsel [Elizabeth M.] Barry. The most important single factor, she adds, is an applicant's high school grades.

Judge [Patrick] Duggan's Dec. 13 [2000], ruling in the undergraduate case sustained the plaintiffs' complaint against the system used when Gratz and Hamacher had been rejected. Duggan said that the "facially different grids and action codes based solely upon an applicant's race" amounted to an "impermissible use of race." But Duggan said the revised system was on the right side of what he called "the thin line that divides the permissible and the impermissible."

Three months later, however, Judge [Bernard] Friedman on March 27 [2001], struck down the law school's admission system. Evidence showed that the school had used a "special admissions" program since 1992 aimed at a minority enrollment of 10 percent to 12 percent.

Friedman relied on a statistical analysis that showed an African-American applicant's relative odds of acceptance were up to 400 times as great as a white applicant's. Friedman rejected the use of diversity to justify the racial preferences, but in any event said the law school's system was not "narrowly tailored" because there was no time limit and there had been no consideration of alternative means of increasing minority enrollment.

The two Michigan cases took on added significance in June [2001], when the

Supreme Court declined for a second time to hear Texas' appeal in the *Hop-wood* case or to hear the plaintiffs' appeal of a ruling by the 9th U.S. Circuit Court of Appeals upholding a discontinued system of racial preferences at the University of Washington Law School. As the lawyers in the Michigan cases prepared for their scheduled appellate arguments, the 11th U.S. Circuit Court of Appeals issued a ruling on Aug. 27 [2001], striking down the University of Georgia's admissions system. With less extensive evidence in the Georgia case, however, legal observers viewed the two Michigan cases as the most likely to be accepted by the Supreme Court for its first full look at race-based admissions since *Bakke*.[1]

1. The Supreme Court decided in June 2003 that the University of Michigan could not use a system that assigned specific points based on race in undergraduate admissions. It could, however, consider race as one of many factors in law school admissions.

Affirmative Action Reduces Discrimination

by Frank H. Wu

About the author: *Frank H. Wu is an associate professor of law at Howard University and the author of* Beyond Black and White.

As a strong supporter of affirmative action, I am often asked to debate the topic. Whether the forum is a television show or a college campus, I always try to decline.

I would like to explain why I do so. A debate is not what we need, and affirmative action is the wrong place to begin. Typically, opponents of affirmative action argue along misleading but effectively divisive lines suggesting that racial quotas benefit unqualified minorities to the detriment of more qualified whites.

Indeed, those of us who support systematic efforts to achieve racial justice can reform the very terms of the discussion. We make a mistake continuing a dispute defined by the other side.

I'd like to offer an alternative framework. I am both more modest and more ambitious than to believe I can persuade people to agree with me on this controversial subject. Instead, I'd like to provoke them into thinking for themselves.

We need new paradigms of civil rights. Rather than engaging in debate, with its angry slogans, rhetorical tricks, and entertainment value, we should strive for dialogue, leading to consensus, and producing action. Serious racial inequalities require a commitment by each of us to what we can do, individually, as well as collectively.

After all, "affirmative action" is only a label given to a wide variety of programs that have been developed as remedies, as a means to an end, in the public and private sectors, voluntarily and through litigation, and out of political compromise. They have in common the use of race to respond to racism. As a matter of constitutional law, their essential feature is that their methods refer to race.

Rather than focusing on affirmative action, we should concentrate on the realities of racial discrimination. Taking up so-called "reverse discrimination" at

Frank H. Wu, "New Thinking About Affirmative Action," *Human Rights*, vol. 26, Summer 1999, pp. 19–22. Copyright © 1999 by the American Bar Association. Reproduced by permission.

the outset shifts our attention away from "the American dilemma," implying incorrectly that the responses to racial bias are the trouble. The better conversation considers three aspects of the issue: problems, principles, and pragmatism.

Problems

First, we must begin where it is proper to begin. The problem is racial discrimination in all its forms. Of course, our society as a whole has made progress within the past generation. Our advances should be neither denied nor taken for granted.

We no longer see the literal signs of legal segregation—"whites only"—of the Jim Crow era.[1] We have reached a basic understanding that stereotypes are unethical. A majority of us support genuine equality of opportunity.

Yet, we continue to face problems of racial bigotry. These wrongs cannot be dismissed as merely theoretical or historical. They are concrete and they are contemporary. By whatever indication of social science or real-life daily experiences, people of color, and especially African Americans, continue to face dissimilar life prospects compared with whites. Whether it is infant mortality, life expectancy, housing segregation, educational outcomes, employment opportunities, or the glass ceiling, virtually every study continues to confirm that there are differences that correlate to race to greater or lesser degrees. While some of these variations can be attributed to a limited extent to class or disadvantage, even controlling for every other factor, people of color, and particularly African Americans, fare worse by objective criteria.

Furthermore, we are beginning to appreciate that racial discrimination can manifest itself in several ways. There is the obvious and the egregious, but there also is the subtle and condoned. Both types deserve our attention.

Extreme situations still persist; shocking incidents continue to occur. We all recognize and condemn the hate crimes, in which people are targeted for violence, even death, on the basis of their skin color. We know that a company that adopts a policy prohibiting the hiring or promotion of minorities is violating a moral norm and settled law. Prosecutions of gruesome murders and civil lawsuit settlements in the hundreds of millions of dollars remind us that notwithstanding all of our progress there regrettably remain individuals and institutions that will practice their prejudices.

We may not realize or be willing to acknowledge the prevalence of the other type of racial bias. It consists of unconscious decisions that have unconscionable consequences. They are actions that are perhaps minor in isolation, but which together generate major effects as a cumulative pattern. It may be racial profiling by government officials, which results in suspicions of African American men who are arrested for traffic violations at rates five times higher

1. Jim Crow was a stereotyped African American from a nineteenth-century song-and-dance act and has come to represent segregation backed by legal enforcement.

than that of the general population. Or it may be a law firm that does not in fact have an explicitly discriminatory policy, but simply has never and does not now have any nonwhite attorneys among its ranks. It is a preference, which many of us share despite ourselves, for people who look like us.

This systematic version of racial discrimination is dangerous and contributes to the anomalous cases. It is structural and forms part of our culture, but its nature renders it much more readily denied. It doesn't take a hardcore racist sitting behind a big desk in a fancy office writing memos stating "No Latinos are allowed here" to send the message that some people are welcome while others don't belong. A specific perpetrator might not be identifiable, and may not actually exist in a classic sense of assigning guilt under the common law, but an injustice may be done and be every bit as harmful.

Principles

Second, we must challenge ourselves to be principled. What is at risk is whether we will all be regarded as stakeholders in an open society. What is at stake is the identity of our institutions, elite and democratic. Our principles conflict. We profess our beliefs in many ideals, sincerely and in good faith, but some of them are mutually incompatible.

Affirmative action reflects the ideals of integration and equality. It is part of a commitment to communities that are racially diverse, egalitarian, and inclusive. It contains the recognition that we share our fate and that coalitions bringing together groups require lasting commitment.

Likewise, color blindness is an aspiration. The risk, however, is that color blindness, as a hope will be confused with color blindness as a reality. We will become blind not to race but to racism.

The color blindness of ideologues is misleading. Anti-affirmative action propagandists promote color blindness as a legal doctrine and not as a moral principle. Writers such as Gary Becker, Richard Epstein, and Clint Bolick wish to prevent the government from recognizing race for remedial purposes. They also defend the right of individuals to rely on race for invidious reasons. They rationalize the latter rule as a consequence of freedom of association or the right to contract.

> *"Affirmative action reflects the ideals of integration and equality. It is part of a commitment to communities that are racially diverse, egalitarian, and inclusive."*

They are recommending the worst of all possible combinations, prohibiting public responses to race but promoting private practices of racism.

Even worse, they are joined by a resurgent trend of pseudo-scientific social Darwinism. These writers confirm the worst racial stereotypes, arguing that they are true and therefore form a proper basis for judgment. For example, Richard Herrnstein and Charles Murray, announced in *The Bell Curve* that

African Americans are genetically inferior with respect to intelligence, and that intelligence determines socioeconomic status. Dinesh D'Souza responded to them in *The End of Racism*, refuting their claim with his own pronouncement that African Americans are culturally pathological, thus dooming themselves by their own behavior to their lot in life. They urge people to practice "rational discrimination," by which it is common sense to assume that African American men are dangerous, criminal, or violent—regardless of the overall consequences of such assumptions.

Merit Comes in Many Forms

Meritocracy also is an aspiration. Its central notions are that people should set high standards and individuals should work hard. Its underlying premise is that rewards are generally distributed fairly; people receive what they deserve, and vice versa.

Yet, affirmative action at its best compels us to realize that merit comes in many forms and the process can be made more fair. Merit does deserve praise. It just shouldn't be circumscribed too rigidly. Few of us would benefit from a rigid competition in which privileges are distributed on the basis of grades and test scores set in high school or even earlier. We all have skills and talents that cannot be measured by quantifiable means. For example, a professional who is willing and able to move or return to an impoverished neighborhood that otherwise would lack medical or legal services is displaying traits that are meritorious.

We can see this at any university. The higher education setting is where affirmative action has been most significant. At any school, even with its general missions of advancing knowledge, teaching, and learning, merit is evaluated in several ways and should be evaluated accordingly. The faculty is a good example. Among the faculty at every school, there are always a few whom the students hate. Students avoid their classes whenever possible, and attendance at their lectures decreases over the semester. These same professors may have won Nobel prizes or Pulitzer prizes, been awarded major grants, or conducted research that is leading to a cure for cancer, or otherwise brought renown to the school. They have merit as scholars, but not as teachers.

There are, those faculty members whom the students love. Students fill their classes to capacity and applaud at the end of their lectures. They have shelves of citations honoring their teaching excellence. These same faculty members, however, may be thought of rather poorly by their academic colleges, or may be utterly unknown because they have published nothing and have developed no original ideas. They have merit as teachers but not as scholars.

None of us is able to excel in each and every dimension of merit. Applying a one-dimensional meaning of merit would result in over emphasis of one of these factors at the expense of the others.

In many contexts, it becomes apparent that a color blind meritocracy isn't what affirmative action opponents support at all. They are inconsistent in their color blindness and selective in their meritocracy. They allow alumni preferences in college admissions, which overwhelmingly benefit whites. Alumni preferences favor "legacies"—children of privileged whites of predominantly Protestant background, whose parents (most likely, fathers) attended Ivy League institutions in an era when they recruited from elite East Coast prep schools, setting maximum limits on Jewish students and enrolling few white ethnics from poor urban origins. At some top universities, the admissions rates for "legacy" children is twice as high as that for the general applicant pool, resulting in many less qualified persons being granted coveted seats in the class. Ironically, while opponents of affirmative action claim it may impose a stigma on beneficiaries, alumni preferences appear to engender the opposite effect of pride. A student can say he is the third generation of the family to matriculate; he is a member of the same dining club as his father; or that building over there is named after his grandfather.

> *"Affirmative action at its best compels us to realize that merit comes in many forms, and the process can be made more fair."*

Incidentally, many supporters of this so-called meritocracy also argue for imposition of maximum quotas on foreign graduate students. They do so based on the stereotype of the calculus teaching assistant who can't speak English. Their efforts are color conscious, as their objections are primarily leveled against nonwhite immigrants. Their efforts are also anti-meritocratic, because it is exactly the possibility of competition from these students that they wish to avoid or limit.

In contrast to groups in competitive conflict and individuals pursuing nothing more than self-interest, affirmative action appeals to the better side of human nature. It suggests that we can cooperate on improvements.

Pragmatism

Third, we must consider policies that work. Pragmatism is an American tradition that applies well to affirmative action. As an intellectual movement, pragmatism has been philosophy applied. It means analyzing the consequences of actions rather than considering abstractions. It forces us to ask whether we would be better off or worse off with each of the options we are presented. It does not depend on false either/or dichotomies, choosing between programs that help now or promises of help deferred.

Pragmatism frames the question. Instead of whether this affirmative action program should be abolished or that affirmative action program should be reformed, we should ask, "what will we do to address racial discrimination?"

We have a series of choices. Considering each in turn makes the case for affirmative action more compelling.

We could do nothing. That would ensure failure. Racial equality will happen neither by accident nor by chance. Racial progress has occurred through a combination of internal and external forces—grassroots civil rights movements and protests coupled with several important Supreme Court decisions and corporate responsibility. Market forces are powerful and can produce amazing results, but eliminating bias does not appear to be among them. Some people have enough of a preference for negative color consciousness that they will pay the price. Exclusion commands a premium.

We could exhort people to be color blind. Such will is necessary but not sufficient by itself. Attitude changes within families and across generations have been crucial to racial reforms. They are not enough though. Lawyers know well that no matter how strongly stated, admonitions are only so many words to be heeded as much in the breech. Rules require enforcement mechanisms.

We could enact legislation forbidding racial discrimination. The many civil rights acts, with their provisions for lawsuits, have served an important function in reducing racial discrimination. They are no panacea. They respond only to cases with "smoking gun" evidence. Litigation is among the least preferable means for resolving society's disputes. It is after-the-fact, complex, contentious, expensive, inefficient, uncertain, and generates additional conflicts.

Affirmative action, then, becomes a much more attractive response. It too is only a partial measure, but it has been effective. Recent studies have proven that racially conscious remedial programs have aided their direct beneficiaries as well as everyone else. They also have confirmed that without the use of race the same outcomes could not have been obtained.

Charles Moskos and John Sibley Butler, two respected sociologists, one white and one black, produced the empirical data that tracked the success of the United States Army in its transition from a segregated military branch formed through conscription to an integrated fighting force made up of volunteers. William Bowen and Derek Bok, former presidents of Princeton and Harvard, respectively, undertook a comprehensive review of college admissions at the most selective institutions throughout the country, over the course of more than a generation.

Both teams of scholars concluded that affirmative action was responsible for the positive transformations of the institutions they examined. They have refuted stereotypes of affirmative action as counterproductive. The beneficiaries themselves have demonstrated, with their accomplishments, that what counts is the content of their character rather than the color of their skin. They have been able to do so only with an opportunity that would not otherwise be available.

The research increasingly is showing that everyone benefits from diversity. In a global economy that is highly competitive, our nation gains nothing if 10 percent of the population is left behind, portrayed with images of inferiority, and sent messages of exclusion. A company or a school that is all white, with no minorities, will not be successful in a diverse democracy.

For all these reasons, affirmative action is just. It deserves to be continued. It can lead to much more.

Affirmative Action Encourages Educational Diversity

by Patricia Gurin, Eric L. Dey, Sylvia Hurtado, and Gerald Gurin

About the authors: *Patricia Gurin is chair of the department of psychology at the University of Michigan. Eric L. Dey is executive associate dean and an associate professor at the University of Michigan school of education. Sylvia Hurtado is associate professor and director of the Center for the Study of Higher and Postsecondary Education at the University of Michigan. Gerald Gurin is a professor and research scientist emeritus at the University of Michigan.*

Educators in U.S. higher education have long argued that affirmative action policies are justified because they ensure the creation of the racially and ethnically diverse student bodies essential to providing the best possible educational environment for students, white and minority alike. Yet until recently these arguments have lacked empirical evidence and a strong theoretical rationale to support the link between diversity and educational outcomes. As Jonathan Alger, former counsel for the American Association of University Professors, argues: "The unfinished homework in the affirmative action debate concerns the development of an articulated vision—supported by a strong evidentiary basis—of the educational benefits of racial diversity in higher education." This suggests not only that educators must clarify the conceptual link between diversity and learning in educational practice, but also that educational researchers play a key role in providing evidence on whether diversity contributes to achieving the central goals of higher education. The purpose of this article is both to provide a theory of how diversity can be linked to educational outcomes in higher education and to test this theory using national data and data from students at the University of Michigan—an institution that has faced affirmative action legal challenges.

In the 1978 case *Regents of the University of California v. Bakke*, U.S. Supreme Court Justice Lewis Powell wrote the pivotal opinion, arguing that the "atmosphere of 'speculation, experiment and creation'—so essential to the quality of higher education—is widely believed to be promoted by a diverse student body. . . . It is not too much to say that the nation's future depends upon leaders trained through wide exposure to the ideas and mores of students as diverse as this Nation of many peoples." Since the *Bakke* decision, the educational benefits of diversity as a compelling governmental interest have provided the primary justification for affirmative action at selective institutions across the country. However, the diversity argument has not been supported in all lower court cases since the original *Bakke* decision. For example, in *Hopwood v. University of Texas*, the Fifth Circuit Court of Appeals denied that diversity has any impact on educational experience: "The use of race, in and of itself, to choose students simply achieves a student body that looks different. Such a criterion is no more rational on its own terms than would be choices based upon the physical size or blood type of applicants." If this statement were true, there would be no basis for arguing that there was a compelling interest in a racially/ethnically diverse student body. However, such a conclusion flies in the face of the role that race and ethnicity have played in our polity and society. As Victor Bolden, David Goldberg, and Dennis Parker point out, "No constitutional compromise was required over blood type; no civil war was fought and no Southern Manifesto signed over physical size."

Educational Diversity Justifies Affirmative Action

Since the *Hopwood* decision, courts across the country have produced conflicting rulings on diversity as a compelling governmental interest. In *Smith v. University of Washington Law School* (2001), the Ninth Circuit Court of Appeals affirmed the district court's ruling that *Bakke* is still good law and stands for the proposition that educational diversity can be a compelling governmental interest that justifies race-sensitive admissions programs. In *Johnson v. Board of Regents of the University of Georgia* (2001), the Eleventh Circuit Court of Appeals declined to rule on the question of whether diversity is a compelling governmental interest but struck down the University of Georgia's admissions policy on the grounds that it was not "narrowly tailored" to that interest. In two cases involving the University of Michigan, one challenging its undergraduate admissions and the other its law school admissions, two different rulings on diversity as a compelling governmental interest were given at the district court level. In *Gratz v. Bollinger, et al.* (2000), the court ruled on summary judgment in favor of the University of Michigan, upholding its current undergraduate admissions policy and finding that diversity was a compelling governmental interest that justified the policy. In *Grutter v. Bollinger, et al.* (2002), the court held that the educational benefits of diversity are not a compelling state interest, and even if they were, the law school's policy was not "narrowly tailored" to the interest of diversity. Both cases were appealed to the Sixth Circuit Court of Appeals, which heard arguments in December 2001. This court overturned the lower court decision in *Grutter*, deciding in favor of the university and setting the stage for an appeal to the U.S. Supreme Court. It is clear from these now-famous higher education cases that the question of whether *Bakke* is still good law and whether diversity is a compelling state interest justifying the use of race-sensitive admissions policies remains controversial. It is also clear that diversity is the primary basis for arguing the constitutionality of using race as one of many factors in college admission, and thus research on *whether* and *how* diversity might affect education is of crucial legal and practical importance.

> *"Affirmative action policies are justified because they ensure . . . diverse student bodies essential to . . . the best possible . . . environment for students, white and minority alike."*

It is important to explain how higher education might expose students to racial and ethnic diversity, since they may experience it in several ways. First, students attend colleges with different levels of racial/ethnic diversity in their student bodies. This has been termed *structural diversity*, or the numerical representation of diverse groups. Although structural diversity increases the probability that students will encounter others of diverse backgrounds, given the U.S. history of race relations, simply attending an ethnically diverse college does not guarantee that students will have the meaningful intergroup interactions that social psychologist Gordon Allport suggested in his classic book, *The Nature of Prejudice*, are important for the reduction of racial prejudice. For this reason, a second definition of racial/ethnic diversity is important, one that involves both the *frequency* and the *quality* of intergroup interaction as keys to meaningful diversity experiences during college, or what we term *informal interaction diversity*. Although these informal interactions with racially diverse peers can occur in many campus contexts, the majority of them occur outside of the classroom. Such interactions may include informal discussions, daily interactions in residence halls, campus events, and social activities. Finally, a third form of diversity experience includes learning about diverse people (content knowledge) and gaining experience with diverse peers in the classroom, or what we term *classroom diversity*. We contend that the impact of racial/ethnic diversity on educational outcomes comes primarily from engagement with diverse peers in the informal campus environment and in college classrooms. Structural diversity is a necessary but insufficient condition for maximal educational benefits; therefore, the theory that guides our study is based on students' actual engagement with diverse peers.

Recent reviews of educational research, as well as summaries of new studies, present an emerging body of scholarship that speaks directly to the benefits of a racially/ethnically diverse postsecondary educational experience. The evidence for the diversity rationale for affirmative action has come from four approaches to research:

1. students' subjective assessments of the benefits they receive from interacting with diverse peers

2. faculty assessments about the impact of diversity on student learning or on other outcomes related to the missions of their universities

3. analyses of monetary and nonmonetary returns to students and the larger community in terms of graduation rates, attainment of advanced and professional degrees that prepare students to become leaders in underserved communities, personal income or other postcollege attainment that results from attending highly selective institutions where affirmative action is critical to achieving diversity

4. analyses tying diversity experience during the college years to a wide variety of educational outcomes

It is important to note that, across these different approaches and different samples of students and faculty, researchers have found similar results showing that a wide variety of individual, institutional, and societal benefits are linked with diversity experiences.

The research reported here is an example of the fourth approach in which we compare how different types of diversity experiences are associated with differences in educational outcomes among students from different racial and ethnic backgrounds. We first present the theoretical foundation for the educational value of racial/ethnic diversity, and then we examine the effects of two kinds of diversity experiences—diversity in the formal classroom and in the informal campus environment—on different educational outcomes.

Racial and ethnic diversity may promote a broad range of educational outcomes, but we focus on two general categories. Learning outcomes include active thinking skills, intellectual engagement and motivation, and a variety of academic skills. Democracy outcomes include perspective-taking, citizenship engagement, racial and cultural understanding, and judgment of the compatibility among different groups in a democracy. The impact of diversity on learning and democracy outcomes is believed to be especially important during the college years because students are at a critical developmental stage, which takes place in institutions explicitly constituted to promote late adolescent development.

Confronting Diversity Encourages Active Thinking

In essays that profoundly affected our understanding of social development, psychologist Erik Erikson introduced the concept of identity and argued that late adolescence and early adulthood are the unique times when a sense of personal and social identity is formed. Identity involves two important elements: a persistent sameness within oneself and a persistent sharing with others. Erikson theorized that identity develops best when young people are given a psychosocial moratorium—a time and a place in which they can experiment with different social roles before making permanent commitments to an occupation, to intimate relationships, to social and political groups and ideas, and to a philosophy of life. We argue that such a moratorium should ideally involve a confrontation with diversity and complexity, lest young people passively make commitments based on their past experiences, rather than actively think and make decisions informed by new and more complex perspectives and relationships.

Institutions of higher education can provide an opportunity for such a psychosocial moratorium, thus supporting young adults through this identity development stage. Residential colleges and universities provide many students with an opportunity to experiment with new ideas, new relationships, and new roles. Peer influences play a normative role in this development, and students are able to explore options and possibilities before making permanent adult commitments. Yet not all institutions of higher education serve this developmental function equally well. Higher education is especially influential when its social milieu is different from students' home and community background and when it is diverse and complex enough to encourage intellectual experimentation and recognition of varied future possibilities. We maintain that attending college in one's home environment or replicating the home community's social life and expectations in a homogeneous college that is simply an extension of the home community impedes the personal struggle and conscious thought that are so important for identity development.

> *"Higher education is especially influential when its social milieu is . . . diverse . . . enough to encourage intellectual experimentation."*

Sociologist Theodore Newcomb's classic study of students at Bennington College supported Erikson's assertion that late adolescence is a time to determine one's relationship to the sociopolitical world and affirmed the developmental impact of the college experience. Newcomb's study demonstrated that political and social attitudes—what Erikson would call one aspect of social identity—are quite malleable in late adolescence and that change occurred particularly in those students to whom Bennington presented new and different ideas and attitudes. Peer influence was critical in shaping the attitudinal changes that Newcomb documented. Follow-ups with these students showed that the attitudes formed during the college experience were quite stable, even twenty-five and fifty years later.

Developmental theorists emphasize that discontinuity and discrepancy spur cognitive growth. Jean Piaget termed this process *disequilibrium.* Drawing on these theories, psychologist Diane Ruble offers a model that ties developmental change to life transitions such as going to college. Transitions are significant because they present new situations about which individuals know little and in which they will experience uncertainty. The early phase of a transition, what Ruble calls construction, is especially important, since people have to seek information in order to make sense of the new situation. Under these conditions individuals are likely to undergo cognitive growth unless they are able to retreat to a familiar world. Ruble's model gives special importance to the first year of college, since it is during this time that classroom and social relationships discrepant from students' home environments become especially important in fostering cognitive growth.

Writing long before the controversies about diversity and affirmative action became politically important or were studied academically, Erikson, Newcomb, and Piaget were not making an explicit case for racial/ethnic diversity. Nonetheless, their arguments about the significance of discontinuity and the power of a late adolescence/early adulthood moratorium provide a strong theoretical rationale for the importance of bringing students from varied backgrounds together to create a diverse and complex learning environment.

Campus environments and policies that foster interaction among diverse students are discontinuous from the home environments of many American students. Because of the racial separation that persists in this country, most students have lived in segregated communities before coming to college. The work of Gary Orfield and associates documents a deepening segregation in U.S. public schools. This segregated precollege educational background means that many students, White and minority alike, enter college without experience with diverse peers. Colleges that diversify their student bodies and institute policies that foster genuine interaction across race and ethnicity provide the first opportunity for many students to learn from peers with different cultures, values, and experiences. Genuine interaction goes far beyond mere contact and includes learning about difference in background, experience, and perspectives, as well as getting to know one another individually in an intimate enough way to discern common goals and personal qualities. In this kind of interaction—in and out of the classroom—diverse peers will learn from each other. This can be viewed as extending the traditional conception of a liberal education as one "intended to break down the narrow certainties and provincial vision with which we are born," [according to the Association of American Colleges and Universities]. . . .

Diversity Enhances Learning

We might expect that a curriculum that deals explicitly with social and cultural diversity and a learning environment in which diverse students interact frequently with one another would affect the content of what is learned. However, based on the recent social psychological research that we discuss below, we consider the less obvious notion that features of the learning environment affect students' modes of thought. In this study we hypothesize that a curriculum that exposes students to knowledge about race and ethnicity acquired through the curriculum and classroom environment and to interactions with peers from diverse racial and ethnic backgrounds in the informal college environment will foster a learning environment that supports active thinking and intellectual engagement.

Research in social psychology over the past twenty years has shown that active engagement in learning and thinking cannot be assumed. This research confirms that much apparent thinking and thoughtful action are actually automatic, or what psychologist Ellen Langer calls mindless. To some extent, mindlessness is the result of previous learning that has become so routine that thinking is unnecessary. Instead, scripts or schemas that are activated and operate automatically guide these learned routines. Some argue that mindlessness is necessary because there are too many stimuli in the world to which to pay attention. It is more efficient for us to select only a few stimuli or, better still, to go on automatic pilot—to be what some people call cognitive misers.

Psychologist John Bargh reviews both historical and recent research evidence showing that automatic psychological processes play a pervasive role in all aspects of everyday thinking. He concludes that automatic thinking is evident not only in perceptual processes (such as categorization) and in the execution of perceptional and motor skills (such as driving and typing), but that it is also pervasive in evaluation, emotional reactions, determination of goals, and social behavior itself. Bargh uses the term *preconscious* to describe processes that act as mental servants to take over from conscious, effortful thinking. One of our tasks as educators is to interrupt these automatic processes and facilitate active thinking in our students.

In one early study indicating the pervasiveness of automatic thinking, Langer described the many positive psychological benefits that people derive from using active, effortful, conscious modes of thought. She also argued that such thinking helps people develop new ideas and ways of processing information that may have been available to them but were simply not often used. In several experimental studies, she showed that such thinking increases alertness and greater mental activity, which fosters better learning and supports the developmental goals of higher education.

> *"A curriculum that exposes students to knowledge about race and ethnicity . . . and to interactions with peers from diverse . . . backgrounds . . . will foster . . . active thinking."*

What are the conditions that encourage effortful, mindful, and conscious modes of thought? Langer contends that people will engage in such modes of thought when they encounter a situation for which they have no script or when the environment demands more than their current scripts provide, such as an encounter discrepant with their past experience. These conditions are similar to what sociologist Rose Coser calls complex social structures—situations where we encounter people who are unfamiliar to us, when these people challenge us to think or act in new ways, when people and relationships change and thus produce unpredictability, and when people we encounter hold different expectations of us. Coser shows that people who function within complex social structures develop a clearer and stronger sense of individuality and a deeper under-standing of the social world.

Diversity Fosters Personal Development

The specific environmental features that Langer and Coser suggest will pro-mote mental activity are compatible with cognitive-developmental theories. In general, those theories posit that cognitive growth is fostered by discontinuity and discrepancy (as in Piaget's notion of disequilibrium). To learn or grow cog-nitively, individuals need to recognize cognitive conflicts or contradictions, sit-uations that, as psychologist Diane Ruble argues, then lead to a state of uncer-tainty, instability, and possibly anxiety. Ruble states:

> Such a state may occur for a number of reasons. . . . It may be generated either
> internally via the recognition of incompatible cognitions or externally during
> social interaction. The latter is particularly relevant to many types of life tran-
> sitions, because such transitions are likely to alter the probability of encounter-
> ing people whose viewpoints differ from one's own.

Racial and ethnic diversity in the student body and university efforts to foster opportunities for diverse students to interact and learn from each other in and out of the classroom offer college students who have grown up in the racially segregated United States the very features that these theories suggest will foster active thinking and personal development. These features include:

• novelty and unfamiliarity that occurs upon the transition to college

• opportunities to identify discrepancies between students with distinct pre-college social experiences

• opportunities to identify discrepancies between students with distinct pre-college social experiences

A White student, evaluating a course on intergroup relations that one of the authors taught at the University of Michigan, conveys the importance of these facets of diversity:

> I come from a town in Michigan where everyone was white, middle-class and
> generally pretty closed-down to the rest of the world, although we didn't think
> so. It never touched us, so I never questioned the fact that we were "normal"
> and everyone else was "different." Listening to other students in the class, es-
> pecially the African American students from Detroit and other urban areas just
> blew me away. We only live a few hours away and yet we live in completely
> separate worlds. Even more shocking was the fact that they knew about "my
> world" and I knew nothing about theirs. Nor did I think that this was even a
> problem at first. I realize now that many people like me can go through life
> and not have to see another point of view, that somehow we are protected
> from it. The beginning for me was when I realized that not everyone shares the
> same views as I, and that our different experiences have a lot to do with that.

One of our primary goals was to discover whether such encounters with diversity contribute to learning outcomes, not only among students at the University of Michigan but also among those attending a variety of four-year institutions across the country. A second key goal was to understand the extent to which these same diversity experiences contribute to the development of the skills and dispositions that students will need to be leaders in a pluralistic democracy.

Diversity Encourages Democracy

From the time the founding fathers debated what form U.S. democracy should take—representational or directly participatory—education has been seen as the key to achieving an informed citizenry. In the compromise they reached involving both representation and broad participation, education was the mechanism that was to make broad participation possible. Benjamin Barber argues that it was [Thomas] Jefferson, certainly no advocate of diversity, who most forcefully argued that broad civic participation required education: "It remained clear to Jefferson to the end of his life that a theory of democracy that is rooted in active participation and continuing consent by each generation of citizens demands a civic pedagogy rooted in the obligation to educate all who would be citizens." To be sure, Jefferson was talking about education for those he defined as the body of citizens and not for the many who were not citizens at that time.

> *"Students educated in diverse institutions will be more motivated and better able to participate in an increasingly heterogeneous and complex society."*

If education is the very foundation of democracy, how do experiences with racial/ethnic diversity affect the process of learning to become citizens? We contend that students educated in diverse institutions will be more motivated and better able to participate in an increasingly heterogeneous and complex society. In *Democratic Education in an Age of Difference*, Richard Guarasci and Grant Cornwell concur, claiming that "community and democratic citizenship are strengthened when undergraduates understand and experience social connections with those outside of their often parochial 'autobiographies,' and when they experience the way their lives are necessarily shaped by others."

However, the compatibility of diversity and democracy is not self-evident. Current critics of multicultural education worry that identities based on race, ethnicity, gender, class, and other categorizations are inimical to the unity needed for democracy. Yet the tension between unity and diversity, however politically charged, is not new in the United States.

In *Fear of Diversity*, Arlene Saxonhouse describes how the pre-Socratic playwrights as well as Plato and Aristotle dealt with the fear that "differences bring on chaos and thus demand that the world be put into an orderly pattern." While Plato envisioned a city in which unity and harmony would be based on the shared characteristics of a homogeneous citizenry, Aristotle recognized the value of heterogeneity and welcomed the diverse. Saxonhouse writes: "Aristotle embraces diversity as the others had not. . . . The typologies that fill almost every page of Aristotle's *Politics* show him uniting and separating, finding underlying unity and significant differences." Aristotle advanced a political theory in which unity could be achieved through differences and contended that democracy based on such a unity would be more likely to thrive than one based on homogeneity. What makes democracy work, according to Aristotle, is equality among citizens (admittedly, in his time only free men, not women or slaves) who hold diverse perspectives and whose relationships are governed by freedom and rules of civil discourse. It is a multiplicity of perspectives and discourses in response to the inevitable conflicts that arise when citizens have differing points of view, not unanimity, that help democracy thrive.

Diversity Teaches That Differences Are Compatible with Unity

Diversity, plurality, equality, and freedom are also implied in Piaget's theory of intellectual and moral development. He argues that children and adolescents can best develop a capacity to understand the ideas and feelings of others—what he calls perspective-taking—and move to a more advanced stage of moral reasoning when they interact with peers who have different points of view. Both differing perspectives and equality in relationships are important for intellectual and moral development. In a homogeneous environment in which young people are not forced to confront the relativity or limitations of their point of view, they are likely to conform to a single perspective defined by an authority. In a hierarchical environment in which young people are not obliged to discuss and argue with others on an equal basis, they are not likely to do the cognitive and emotional work that is required to understand how other people think and feel. These cognitive and emotional processes promote the moral development needed to make a pluralistic democracy work.

In the United States, however, common conceptions of democracy do not treat difference as being compatible with unity. In general, popular understandings of democracy and citizenship take one of two forms: 1) a liberal individualist conception in which citizens participate by voting for public servants to represent them and by other individual acts, and 2) a direct participatory conception in which people from similar backgrounds who are familiar with each other come together to debate the common good, as in the New England town meeting. Both of these conceptions privilege individuals and similarities rather than groups and differences.

The increasingly heterogeneous U.S. population challenges these popular conceptions of democracy. Consequently, we are now facing cultural, academic, and political debates over the extent to which American democracy can survive increasing heterogeneity and group-based social and political claims. Yet, it is clear that an ethnic hierarchy or one-way assimilation, both of which call for muting differences and cultural identities, is much less likely to prevail than in the past.

The theories of Aristotle and Piaget both suggest that difference and democracy can be compatible. The conditions deemed important for this compatibility include the presence of diverse others and diverse perspectives, equality among peers, and discussion according to rules of civil discourse. We hypothesize that these conditions foster the orientations that students will need to be citizens and leaders in the postcollege world: perspective-taking, mutuality and reciprocity, acceptance of conflict as a normal part of life, capacity to perceive differences and commonalties both within and between social groups, interest in the wider social world, and citizen participation.

Affirmative Action Is Necessary to Build the Black Middle Class

by Rufus G.W. Sanders

About the author: *Rufus G.W. Sanders is a contributing editor and columnist for the* Black Business Journal, *a monthly magazine devoted to national and international news of interest to the black business community.*

Affirmative Action has worked for the last 30 years to create a Black middle class. It has helped to integrate the American society and to truly diversify the American culture. It also has served to help nurture the socialization and the psychosocial development of Black people in this country. It was through affirmative education that Black people finally were able to assimilate into the American mainstream; but now the president wants to end the one social program in the history of America that even came close to the closing of the gaps of racism. No other program has had as much success. . . . Affirmative Action is about attempts to bring historically underrepresented groups who have suffered discrimination into a higher degree of participation within the society. Affirmative Action attempts to remedy some of the vileness by allowing for opportunity, chance and redress of being historically taken advantage of by the state all because of the color of one's skin. [George W.] Bush has proposed nothing to replace the progress of Affirmative Action. While he certainly is no visionary, he still must be aware of the tremendous strides that have been made because of the bold action taken by the Affirmative Action Program.

Initially, I was shocked when the President George W. Bush announced that he would file a Supreme Court brief to end Affirmative Action. [No brief had been filed as of July 2003.] On second thought, I probably shouldn't have been. Recall that, after all, he's the son of the president George Herbert Walker Bush who refused for two years to sign the Civil Rights Act of 1991. You know the act that only wanted to restore and strengthen the civil rights laws of 1964 and

1968 which had banned discrimination in both employment and housing. The younger Bush follows the Republican right wing manifesto. We recall, too that his hero, President Ronald Reagan, in the mid-1980s refused to sign the Civil Rights Act of 1982.

With Bush's January 2003 statement, deliberately misusing and twisting affirmative action to mean "racial quotas", I am convinced that like most of the dominant American population, he is not only racially insensitive but also in denial about the true American racial condition. Bush fails to understand the true historical and psychological dynamics of cultural racism and suffers from all the residuals of white privilege.

It was reported at the 2002 State of the Black World Conference that in the United States, though the walls of legal segregation have been abolished and multitudes of Black faces are

"Affirmative Action has worked for the last 30 years to create a Black middle class."

now in elective office, especially in rural areas of the Southern sections of the U.S., the vestiges of institutional racism remain painfully intact. Black farmers continue to lose land at an alarming rate and the urban ghettos resemble "domestic colonies."

They are nothing but disempowered zones of desolation, despair and nihilism where Black people still suffer from the ravages of ongoing poverty and political neglect. While Black people have made progress as middle class citizens and have become upward mobile; not much of the progress or the middle classness has translated into real economic and political power for the masses of Black people.

Blacks Continue to Play Catch Up

This seems to be the piece that the dominant culture just can't seem to get. The key reason being, of course, that in the White equation for Black success have always seem to intentionally ignore that one embarrassing variable—the 400 years of involuntary servitude called slavery, as well as just how extremely difficult it is for Blacks to play catch up after only about 40 years of legal desegregation. What the powers that be won't do is to talk honestly about the living legacies of structural racism. What we need in this country is open and frank dialogue about the historical origins and meaning of race in this society, and how we must begin to overcome the many maligning residuals of the institutional. This would begin the process of uprooting and deconstructing the structures of white privilege which forms the very floor boards of American racism.

Every day white Americans wake up to the feeling that they are entitled to the best treatment, better life quality, better educational and job opportunities simply because they are Americans—white Americans. They have higher rates of home ownership, longer life expectancies, greater economic opportunities, larger personal net worth, and assured protection by the police and court systems. As professor Manning Marable has said, "It's woven into the fabric of white daily living." If Blacks are truly Americans then they should also awake with the same feelings of white euphoria but they don't.

Blacks continue to face psychological hurdles and significant challenges that linger from the horrific Jim Crow legacy of institutional segregation. They worry on a daily basis about racial profiling, police brutality, tougher criminal sentencing, and more prisons, fleeting educational opportunities, economic dependency, and the death penalty and so on.

It was because of the cultural context of the Black experience that Affirmative Action was created in the first place, not to mention that it was really a way to deal with white guilt which had become internalized.

President G.W. Bush must know that in any multiracial community where democracy is elusive, the tyranny of the majority can be most crippling, especially when it is based upon the competitive forces of capitalism.

Rather than inspire us and lead us into discussions on how we can create the "beloved Community," the president continues to socially divide us by misappropriating terms such as quotas, set asides, reverse discrimination, and preferential treatment. He never once mentions the chronically deprived communities, or the remaining discrimination in education, hiring practices or economic disparities that are yet part of this democracy.

Therefore, I ask the question: if not Affirmative Action programs exactly, what is it that Bush proposes to do about the lingering effects of discrimination. Reparations[1] maybe?

---

1. Reparations are payments that some people believe should be given to African Americans as recompense for years of slavery and discrimination.

Affirmative Action Helps Make American Business More Competitive

by Christopher M. Leporini

About the author: *Christopher M. Leporini is a Chicago-based freelance writer.*

Corporate affirmative action deserves a distinct place in America's continuing dialogue on race, gender and inequality. In recent years, the affirmative action debate has focused on government-sponsored affirmative action and university admissions, leaving corporate affirmative action relatively unexamined. This oversight is significant, because affirmative action's future remains uncertain. The 1994 Republican revolution weakened affirmative action advocates' political clout, reducing political support from Capitol Hill. Several pending court cases and voter initiatives could potentially eliminate many forms of affirmative action. But corporate programs are distinct from government-sponsored affirmative action in ways that substantially increase their chances of survival.

The majority of corporate affirmative action programs are voluntary attempts to improve workforce diversity. They are unaffected by thorny constitutional issues, such as those raised by the lawsuit against the University of Michigan, which plague university admissions programs.[1] Jennifer Gratz, a white student, alleges the university's affirmative action program denied her admission based on her race, even through she was qualified. Terry Pell, senior counsel for the Center for Individual Rights, makes a clear distinction between the Michigan case and voluntary corporate affirmative action. The Washington D.C.-based public interest law firm is suing the university on behalf of Ms. Gratz. He argues that the purpose of the university program is irrelevant, because it violates

---

1. In June 2003 the U.S. Supreme Court decided that the University of Michigan could not use a system that assigned specific points based on race in undergraduate admissions. Jennifer Gratz was denied admission under this point system.

the Fourteenth Amendment. "If affirmative action is illegal and unconstitutional, it doesn't matter whether it serves a purpose," Pell said.

Corporate programs, however, don't face this kind of legal challenge. Still, corporate affirmative action suffers from a public perception problem. Its nature is often misunderstood, because people do not make distinctions between types of affirmative action. According to Harvard University Professor of Sociology Barbara Reskin, the popular belief that affirmative action means quotas is unfounded. "What people object to doesn't exist," Reskin said; "quotas are illegal, except under special circumstances as a court-prescribed remedy."

Corporate affirmative action encompasses a wide range of strategies often not recognized as affirmative action. These programs include aggressive outreach to women and minorities, including recruitment and mentoring programs. Kraft Food's Management Development programs successfully implemented this strategy. In 1994 Kraft's managerial representation of women increased, despite an overall management workforce reduction. Silicon

> *"Businesses are attempting to sell their products to diverse markets, and having a diverse workforce can only aid this goal."*

Graphics, Inc., a California technology company, also utilizes these kinds of comprehensive diversity initiatives. "Management training sessions are designed to help managers bridge communication gaps they might not even realize exist," said Silicon Graphics Director of Diversity Initiatives, Deborah Dagit. Inclusion training helps managers to recognize how factors such as race and gender can affect relations between coworkers. These programs, however, also address other issues that can affect work performance, including assertiveness and personality conflicts.

"Having a more diverse team leads to greater innovation and creativity as well as opening up the possibilities of different perspectives," Dagit said. This is one of a number of benefits that companies report from affirmative action programs. Another benefit is the forging of comfortable customer relationships. Businesses are attempting to sell their products to diverse markets, and having a diverse workforce can only aid this goal.

"When implemented seriously, affirmative action programs can have a profound influence on offering women and minorities opportunities," said Helen Norton, Director of Legal and Public Policy for the National Partnership for Women and Families. While the glass ceiling still exists to some extent, Norton acknowledges, it would be far worse without these types of programs. Less than 5% of senior managers in Fortune 1000 companies are women and minorities, according to the fact-finding report issued by the Federal Glass Ceiling Commission in 1995. These numbers are far disproportionate to the groups' representation in the workforce. Women comprise 46% of the total workforce, and minorities comprise 21%. The commission endorsed corporate affirmative action as a tool to fully utilize a diverse labor force and maintain a competitive presence in the global economy.

Some workers resent the intrusions they feel diversity programs impose on them. Norton attributes this to inadequate communication of goals by managers. In fact, the problem may be more complex. Opponents of affirmative action are motivated by a wide range of concerns. Some believe that it runs contrary to the idea of equality, while others feel that it furthers the perception that minorities cannot succeed without special help.

Survey results show that Americans are deeply divided over affirmative action. According to Princeton University Politics Professor Jennifer Hochschild, a number of factors may influence these national survey results, including the way the interviewer introduces her/himself and the order of questions asked in the survey. Loaded terms such as quotas, preferences, and reverse discrimination tend to produce inflammatory results. "Although these factors can serve to undermine the credibility of an individual survey, collectively they give a pretty good sense of how people feel about affirmative action," Hochschild said. Barbara Reskin also argues that the grass roots opposition to affirmative action portrayed by the news media doesn't exist. She described the disparity between news stories about support for affirmative action and the truth as "mind blowing." Reskin cited surveys as evidence that support for affirmative action has remained stable over the past 20 years.

Public opinion has taken on a particular importance in light of California's Proposition 209, which banned state-sponsored affirmative action. The U.S. Supreme Court recently upheld the proposition's constitutionality, opening the door for similar bills to appear in other states. However, as the experiences of Silicon Graphics and other California companies demonstrate, affirmative action can persist in the corporate world, even after it is abandoned by government. "This decision has not lessened our company's commitment to affirmative action," Dagit said. In fact, though Silicon Graphics is required to practice affirmative action because the company's business involves government contracting, its efforts extend beyond the minimum mandated by federal law.

Strong corporate support for affirmative action programs makes it likely that such programs will persist, even in the absence of government support. In the final analysis affirmative action can prove beneficial to a company's bottom line. "We are in a strong economy where corporations are competing for quality workers" says Norton, "and the majority of new entrants into the labor markets are women and minorities." Diversity programs can help businesses maintain competitiveness in vying for these labor resources. A 1994 survey of corporate executives found that 38% of executives saw diversity initiatives as a competitive issue, and almost half said it was a business need. Only 4% gave social responsibility as the reason for encouraging diversity. Ultimately, corporate affirmative action may survive primarily as a function of our increasingly global and diverse economy.

Affirmative Action Is No Longer Necessary

by the *Economist*

About the author: *The* Economist *is an international daily newspaper covering economics, business, and politics.*

The latest struggle in America's two decades of anguish over racial preferences is grinding towards a possible conclusion. The Supreme Court [in early April 2003] heard the most significant race-discrimination case for a generation.[1] Emotions are running high on both sides of the debate. Despite this, the court should not merely tinker with the concept of affirmative action, as it has done in the past. It should boldly rule out the use of race as a factor in university admissions, setting aside an outdated idea which is now doing America more harm than good.

In 1997, three white students with good marks were denied places at the University of Michigan, one at its law school. All three sued the university for discrimination, arguing that academically less-qualified black and Hispanic students were admitted instead. In deciding their cases, the Supreme Court's nine justices will rule whether universities, public or private, may continue to discriminate on the basis of race. Twenty-five years ago, the court forbade the use of explicit racial quotas but offered the idea that race could nevertheless be used as a "plus factor" in considering aspiring students.

That logical fudge left the door open to racial preferences which all too often work exactly like quotas. The University of Michigan's programme—which weighs skin colour even more heavily than standardised-test scores—is merely one of the more extreme examples. Others use less explicit, but equally discriminatory, formulas. Though all of America's top universities deny having a racial quota, this is what their policies amount to in all but name.

---

1. As of this writing, the Supreme Court limited, but did not eliminate, affirmative action in university admissions.

Affirmative action's original rationale was to redress past racial wrongs. This made sense. America's blacks were victimised first by slavery and then a century of legal, and frequently violent, discrimination. They could not be expected to shed immediately the shackles of the past, and to compete without help for places at university and the best jobs. But affirmative action was only really justified as a temporary measure. Nearly 40 years after America's landmark civil rights act, the time has come to live up to the ideal of race neutrality.

Instead, affirmative action has become a permanent feature of American life. Now its rationale, supported not only by America's top universities, but also most of its large companies and even its military, is the pursuit of "diversity". But this is a poor argument for making racial discrimination a permanent evil.

The most recent census shows the old black-white divide breaking down in America. A larger fraction of Americans than ever say they belong to more than one race. Should the offspring of Tiger Woods, a multiracial golfer and millionaire, be eligible for racial preferences? Today there are more "Hispanics", a racial category invented in America which also benefits from affirmative action, than blacks. In five or six decades, whites may be a minority. Should they too then become eligible for affirmative action?

> *"The time for affirmative action has passed. A majority of Americans say they oppose using skin colour to allocate university places and jobs."*

Of course not. Defenders of racial preferences paint a bleak picture of a world without affirmative action. But there are many other ways of fostering diversity while treating each person as an individual rather than as a representative of a racial group. Universities should still be free to take students' backgrounds into account: whether, for example, they come from a poor home, or have surmounted personal obstacles. California's universities, where racial preferences were banned in the 1990s, have used such schemes to create diverse student bodies without using race.

It is a pity that elite universities have become the focal point for America's racial rancour. For this obscures the real place where discrimination occurs: through woefully inadequate education for huge numbers of poor minority students. Fixing this problem is less glamorous and more difficult than engineering the ethnic mix at elite colleges and law schools, but it would help far more people.

The time for affirmative action has passed. A majority of Americans say they oppose using skin colour to allocate university places and jobs. Across the world, in India, Malaysia, South Africa, and Brazil, racial preferences have caused needless strife. America's Supreme Court should send a message to the world that it takes seriously the words of its constitution, which affords "equal protection of the laws" to all its people. Racial preferences are an affront to this principle, the foundation stone of any decent society.

Encouraging Educational Diversity Is Not a Legitimate Justification for Affirmative Action

by Roger Clegg

About the author: *Roger Clegg is general counsel for the Center for Equal Opportunity, a conservative think tank focused on issues concerning racial preferences, immigration and assimilation, and multicultural education.*

We hear a lot about diversity these days. Colleges declare that they celebrate diversity and strive for a diverse student body. Companies hire diversity consultants and fall all over themselves in professing that diversity is good business.

It's hard to be against diversity. Who in America would speak out for uniformity or homogeneity, let alone monotony or sameness?

Nonetheless, I'm sick of diversity. Not because I have anything against non-European Americans in our colleges or workplaces. Let's be honest: Despite the unsubtle hints of the pro-diversity crowd, almost no one is arguing along those lines anymore.

The opposite of being pro-diversity is not being anti-diversity. It's being diversity-indifferent, and that's me. My T-shirt would not say "Diversity Sucks." It would say "Diversity—Who Cares?"

Why am I sick of all the praise for diversity? Because it cloaks an agenda that is anti-merit, pro-preference, and anti-assimilationist.

As the Jim Crow era[1] fades into the past, the rise of new discrimination to make up for old discrimination becomes increasingly hard to justify. So those committed to preferences based on race and ethnicity have had to come up with another

---

1. Jim Crow was a stereotyped African American from a nineteenth-century song-and-dance act and has come to represent segregation backed by legal enforcement.

approach—one that has nothing to do with present or past discrimination.

For that, diversity is perfect. It's an excuse for preferences that can last forever. But if a touchy-feely rationale like diversity is compelling enough to justify racial discrimination, then anything is.

The diversity-mongers want higher education to make special efforts to achieve some predetermined racial and ethnic mix. The mix that would naturally occur if people were selected on their merits isn't good enough. In other words, colleges and universities should develop preferences—that is, discriminate—in favor of the underrepresented and against the overrepresented.

Diversity proponents give two basic rationales for their views—rationales that, incidentally, contradict each other. The first one holds that a focus on diversity helps people see that race and ethnicity don't matter: Good students, faculty members, and administrators come in all colors. That makes sense only if the different individuals admitted or hired have the same qualifications. For example, if you're expecting to teach white students that black students are just as good academically as the white students are, you had better be sure that the black students that you admit really are on a par with the white students. Otherwise, you won't erode bigotry—you'll reinforce it.

The sad truth, however, is that as colleges give pluses to certain races and ethnic groups in an attempt to achieve diversity, they are, by definition, selecting those who would not have been chosen on the merits. It's difficult to convince people that skin color and ancestry don't matter when everyone knows that you are deliberately considering them.

The other rationale contends just the opposite: We should make greater strides toward diversity precisely *because* of the differences among races and ethnic groups. Diversity is important, this argument goes, because those with different skin color and ancestry have different insights and perspectives as well.

Does anyone really believe that? Does anyone really believe, for instance, that all Asian-Americans, but only Asian-Americans, share certain vast quantities of knowledge? I'm prepared to believe that women will never quite understand some things about men, and that men won't ever understand some things about women. But I draw the line at "It's a black thing, you wouldn't understand."

Go ahead and try me, I say. I have a pretty good imagination. Most people who use the "you wouldn't understand" line aren't willing to try to explain it, because they know, deep down, that it doesn't make any sense.

> *"The diversity-mongers want higher education to make special efforts to achieve some predetermined racial and ethnic mix."*

Skin color does not equal ideas, and ethnicity does not equal experiences. The position to the contrary used to be called stereotyping. Moreover, since the invention of the printing press, it has not been necessary to meet people in order to learn their perspectives. And show me a college where most of the learning results from exposure to other students, and I'll show you an institution that isn't worth the tuition it charges. You will see more real diversity by working a summer at a blue-collar job—and you'll get paid for it.

Speaking of the workplace, discrimination is not justified on the basis of diversity there, either. Having a particular color or ethnicity might be advantageous in some isolated circumstances: Perhaps a Mexican-American recruiter for a college will do better than an Anglo at attracting students from a predominantly Mexican-American high school. But not always. And for those who use such an argument, does that mean it's OK to give a preference to the Anglo woman so that she can recruit at Anglo schools? No, I didn't think so.

> *"Diversity is one of those things, like falling in love, that works only when it comes naturally. It cannot and should not be forced."*

For most jobs, and most disciplines, it's irrelevant whether someone is of a particular racial or ethnic background. Do we ever speak of black mathematics, Asian chemistry, or Hispanic economics? Of course not. The situations in which one's ethnicity or race really makes a difference are few and far between. When we exaggerate the number of those situations, we engage in nothing more than sloppy stereotyping.

If colleges and universities lower standards to achieve diversity in admissions, diversity advocates will inevitably pressure those institutions to rig the requirements in grading and for graduation. After that, diversity advocates will move on to the college workplace and start questioning how institutions determine who gets promoted. And so on. All this in the face of the statutes that make it illegal to discriminate against anyone on the basis of race or ethnicity.

Implicit in the praise for diversity is the notion that we shouldn't have rules or standards, and shouldn't require people from other cultures to conform to them. That is ethnocentrism, we are told.

Some folks have cultures that are louder and more obnoxious—excuse me, less inhibited—than others, and we must accept them all. Being on time and being polite are less important to some groups, you see. And heaven forbid that we would require people to speak English, let alone proper English, in school or college. That would have a disparate impact on people of some national origins—which violates civil-rights laws.

Finally, we cannot expect individuals from some racial and ethnic groups to do well on timed, paper-and-pencil tests. They will perform better building something with Legos and displaying interpersonal skills, an approach used in an admissions test that some selective institutions are considering.

Such arguments are not only condescending, they're wrong. It's fine to eat different kinds of food and to have pride in one's ancestors. But in matters of language and our civic culture—as well as, more broadly, our manners and morality—assimilation should be the goal. An America that is multiracial and multiethnic, yes. Multicultural, no. *E pluribus unum:* Out of many, one.

To assert that we need more diversity is just another way of saying that we have too many members of groups that we'll have to start setting quotas for. Without a concerted push for uniform diversity (a nice oxymoron), many colleges will undoubtedly have "too many" Jewish students and "not enough" black students, "too many" Hispanic faculty members and "not enough" Asian faculty members. But that's not the end of the world. Diversity is one of those things, like falling in love, that works only when it comes about naturally. It cannot and should not be forced.

When we impose diversity upon an institution, we create resentment and stigmatization, break the law, compromise a college's mission, and tell some people that they aren't going to be admitted or hired or promoted, because they have the wrong melanin content or ancestry.

Whatever the dubious benefits of diversity, is it worth all that?

Affirmative Action Is Not Necessary to Help Build the Black Middle Class

by Larry Elder

About the author: *Larry Elder is a writer, attorney, and host of the nationally syndicated radio program,* The Larry Elder Show. *He is also the author of* Confronting Bias, Lies, and the Special Interests That Divide America.

Senator Trent Lott, in an ultimately failed effort to salvage his career as incoming Senate majority leader, appeared on BET [Black Entertainment Television] and announced his support for "affirmative action." Not only, said the senator, does he support affirmative action, but he also "practices it" by hiring minorities.

Lott's ill-advised remarks at Strom Thurmond's birthday party[1] place the administration in an awkward position. The University of Michigan, in a case currently before the Supreme Court[2] and about which the administration has yet to take a position,[3] argues that its affirmative action program accomplishes "diversity," in and of itself a "compelling state interest."

Few argue against "outreach," casting a wide net to ensure awareness of and opportunities for the qualified. But preferences, the kind of affirmative action practiced by the University of Michigan, lowers standards to achieve racial diversity, thus discriminating against the more qualified.

The Detroit News found that the racial preferences policies of seven Michigan colleges and universities resulted in a disturbing pattern. Many minority students dropped out at a much higher rate, presumably because of lowered standards for admission. "Among black students," said *The Detroit News*, "who

1. Senator Lott commented that the segregationist policies of Senator Strom Thurmond should have been made the law of the land.   2. As of this writing, the U.S. Supreme Court limited, but did not eliminate, affirmative action in university admissions.   3. The administration of President George W. Bush did not take a position on this decision.

were freshmen in 1994, just 40 percent got their diplomas after six years, compared to 61 percent of white students and 74 percent of Asians. . . . The state's universities have special programs aimed at helping black students meet financial, social and academic challenges, but graduation rates for blacks haven't improved consistently over the past decade, the *News* found. . . . Universities knowingly admit students who have a high chance of failing."

> *"The growth of the black middle class long predates the adoption of race-conscious social policies."*

Secretary of State Colin Powell distinguished preferences from affirmative action in his autobiography. "Equal rights and equal opportunity . . . mean just that," said Powell. "They do not mean preferential treatment. Preferences, no matter how well intended, ultimately breed resentment among the nonpreferred. And preferential treatment demeans the achievements that minority Americans win by their own efforts. The present debate over affirmative action has a lot to do with definitions. If affirmative action means programs that provide equal opportunity, then I am all for it. If it leads to preferential treatment or helps those who no longer need help, I am opposed."

Affirmative Action Did Not Help the Black Middle Class Grow

But haven't preferences played a key role in the economic growth of blacks?

In "America in Black and White," Stephan and Abigail Thernstrom demonstrated that the black middle class grew well before affirmative action. Nor did affirmative action accelerate the pace of the black middle class. "The growth of the black middle class long predates the adoption of race-conscious social policies," said the Thernstroms. "In some ways, indeed, the black middle class was expanding more rapidly before 1970 than after. . . . Many of the advances black Americans have made since the Great Depression occurred before anything that can be termed 'affirmative action' existed. . . . In the years since affirmative action (the black middle class) has continued to grow but not at a more rapid pace than in the preceding three decades, despite a common impression to the contrary."

Robert Johnson, the founder of Black Entertainment Television, recently became the first minority to own a majority stake in a major sports franchise. "I wouldn't want to go into a league saying I got my franchise because I'm a minority," said Johnson, "or because I got a discount to what the next guy paid. . . . The last thing you want to do is be in the room because you got a set-aside. There's no way that I am looking for a guaranteed outcome just because of my minority status."

Hard work wins. This is precisely how blacks achieved their success. With an economy of half a trillion a year, the black GDP [Gross Domestic Product], were it a separate country, would place in the top 15 nations in the world.

In 1901, three decades after the emancipation, [African American educator]

Booker T. Washington said, "When a Negro girl learns to cook, to wash dishes, to sew, to write a book, or a Negro boy learns to groom horses, or to grow sweet potatoes, or to produce butter, or to build a house, or to be able to practise (sic) medicine, as well or better than some one else, they will be rewarded regardless of race or colour (sic). In the long run, the world is going to have the best, and any difference in race, religion, or previous history will not long keep the world from what it wants.

"I think that the whole future of my race hinges on the question as to whether or not it can make itself of such indispensable value that the people in the town and the state where we reside will feel that our presence is necessary to the happiness and well-being of the community. No man who continues to add something to the material, intellectual, and moral well-being of the place in which he lives is long left without proper reward. This is a great human law which cannot be permanently nullified."

Affirmative Action Ignores Individual Merit

by Shelby Steele

About the author: *Shelby Steele is a research fellow at the Hoover Institution, a conservative think tank.*

The affirmative action debate comes to us every season in a different guise. Recently—as if to illustrate the degree to which race has corrupted the practice of social science in America—Derek Bok and William Bowen used their Ivy League imprimatur (they are, respectively, the former presidents of Harvard and Princeton) to assert that "the data" showed preferential treatment for blacks and Hispanics in college admissions to be a great success. So "the data" became accepted as fact until people like Stephan and Abigail Thernstrom showed that "the data" in this case constituted a mask. When, for example, a survey that found that black students were happy with their college experience was used to dismiss the complex matter of blacks being stigmatized by racial preferences, it was clear that "the data" really meant, as T.S. Eliot said in another context, preparing "a face to meet the faces that you meet."

This season's affirmative action debate seems to be shaping up as an argument over the meaning and relevance of merit. For decades racial preferences in college admissions have effectively preserved higher standards of merit for whites and Asians by lowering standards for blacks and Hispanics. Academic merit, as the quality most prized by universities, could go relatively undisturbed as long as it did not prevent schools from bringing in more blacks and Hispanics.

But now that court decisions are making it clear that universities (and society in general) will have to move away from racial preferences, it is also clear that merit stands in the way of diversity. On average, black students from families earning $70,000 and up do worse on the SAT than whites from families in the lowest income bracket. Without a racial preference, blacks and Hispanics must compete unaided in an academic contest that can only be decided on merit.

Thus, diversity suddenly requires a direct assault on merit. Merit must be weakened and relativized as a principle. Its decisiveness must be recast as un-fairness. And most of all, it must be smothered in sophistications. What is merit really? Isn't academic ability only "one kind" of merit? Should higher educa-tion "referee" opportunity? Today, the educational establishment finds itself de-voted to an odd kind of innovation: schemes in which the mechanism of social inclusion is tolerance for academic mediocrity.

One such scheme, the new "strivers" formula for the SAT developed by the Educational Testing Service, would effectively handicap students by race and social disadvantage. The more markers of disadvantage a student has—the number and kind of electrical appliances in the home is one such marker—the more points are deducted from a projected score. When a student scores 200 points over this obviously low concocted score, he is designated a "striver"—someone with more potential than his actual score reveals.

If this formula errs by using dubious arithmetic to arrive at a judgment of hu-man potential, its worse offense is to count being black, by itself, as a handicap. In fact, unless blackness is thrown into the calculation, this formula fails to bring in the desired number of blacks.

Tolerance for Mediocrity Is Becoming the Norm

Fortunately, the strivers proposal has met widespread criticism, most recently from the president of the College Board. But tolerance of mediocrity as the mechanism of inclusion is nonetheless fast becoming the norm. Thus, accord-ing to guidelines issued [in 1999] by the U.S. Department of Education, if stan-dardized tests have a "disparate impact" on minorities (that is, if minorities do poorly on them), then schools that use them may be in violation of civil rights laws—as if laws designed to protect black freedom were also intended to pro-tect black mediocrity. Similarly, Texas and California have developed plans that make the top 10 percent or 4 percent, respectively, of every high school's grad-uating class eligible for admission to the state's most selective schools. Neither state considered such schemes until racial preferences were no longer available.

All these ingenious assaults on merit suggest a loss of faith in a racial equal-ity grounded in merit—in comparable levels of competence and skill between the races. They effectively sever racial equality from merit in order to engineer equality between unequals. But, even more than faithlessness, there is a certain desperation in this. Where does it come from?

It comes, I believe, from the mid-1960s victories of the civil rights movement, which among other things caused American institutions to suffer a great loss of moral authority. Guilty of pre-serving white privilege for centuries, these institutions now had to prove they were not racist in order to function in a society profoundly shamed by its

> *"Only a rigorous and unbending adherence to the principle of merit would give us a shot at real equality."*

racism. This need to prove a negative—on pain of being stigmatized as racist—bred the desperation that, in turn, led to the two great themes of racial reform since the '60s: deference and license.

Policies of Deference and License Were Destructive

To reclaim their lost moral authority, institutions had to offer policies to blacks (and other minorities) that deferred to their history of victimization and gave them a license not to meet the same standards and expectations as others. The result was a welfare system that asked nothing at all from its impoverished recipients—no work, no educational development, no family responsibility, nothing. Following quickly thereafter came deference and license for the black middle class in the form of racial preferences.

The separation of racial equality from merit, the assault on merit in the name of black inclusion, the engineering of an "equality" between unequal groups—all this is the inevitable fallout of racial reform based on a trade of deference and license to blacks for moral authority to whites. But the civil rights victories left black America with a very different goal than larger America. We did not need moral redemption from a racist past; we needed to develop the skills that would make us competitive with others and to further embrace the value system that would help us do that. We needed to ask more of ourselves, not less. Only a rigorous and unbending

> *"The 'inclusion' we most need now is in the realm of intellectual respect—which can be gained through merit alone."*

adherence to the principle of merit would give us a shot at real equality.

Instead, what we got from the great and powerful institutions around us was deference and license. This seduced us into a void where nothing much was expected and where failure brought few consequences save more government money—where all incentives pressed toward inertia. Single-parent homes, gangs in the neighborhood, poor schools—things that can be overcome when a nation-building ethic prevails—became immutable barriers that actually excused us from overcoming. We bought into a liberalism that subsidized our inertia as it sought to redeem the moral authority of American institutions.

And now we get a "strivers" SAT formula and 10 percent and 4 percent plans that open up an avenue toward acceptable mediocrity. I can only hope that we are coming into an era—after so much failure—when moral authority goes to institutions only when they approach minorities in a spirit of expectation and consequences rather than deference and license. It is no coincidence that black excellence, even superiority, is so visible in those areas where we live by high expectations and enforced consequences—sports, music, entertainment, literature. The "inclusion" we most need now is in the realm of intellectual respect—which can be gained through merit alone.

Chapter 4

Do Efforts to Prevent Terrorism Threaten Civil Rights?

Chapter Preface

A little more than a month after the September 11, 2001, terrorist attacks on America, Congress passed the USA PATRIOT (Uniting and Strengthening America by Providing Appropriate Tools Required to Intercept and Obstruct Terrorism) Act. This 342-page law creates vast new powers for law enforcement in the areas of search and surveillance, and expands the powers of the attorney general and secretary of state to designate groups, including entire religious groups, as terrorist organizations. Under the new law the attorney general also has the power to detain noncitizens indefinitely without charging them with a crime, and to deport naturalized citizens without a trial. Further, at the attorney general's discretion, the names of those detained and the proceedings against them may be kept secret.

Conceived by the Bush administration as a necessary response to terrorism, supporters of the act maintain that the USA PATRIOT Act strikes a fair balance between the need to keep the country secure from terrorism and the need to protect civil rights. According to Senator Orrin G. Hatch, chairman of the U.S. Senate Judiciary Committee, "Nothing in the PATRIOT Act threatens our cherished Bill of Rights. . . . Moreover, despite the steady drumbeat of opposition by some groups, none of them has cited one instance of abuse against our constitutional rights, nor one shred of evidence to contradict the fact that these tools have saved American lives by preventing terrorist attacks against our people." Attorney General John Ashcroft concurs, noting that the PATRIOT Act has helped the Justice Department identify hundreds of suspected terrorists. "Our ability to prevent an additional terrorist attack in the United States would be more difficult, if not impossible, without the PATRIOT Act. The PATRIOT Act gave us the tools we need."

However, the act's critics point out that despite the importance and complexity of the USA PATRIOT Act, it was hastily written and passed with little debate. Argues columnist David Cole in the *Nation*, "The nuts and bolts of the law were worked out in a couple of all-night sessions and approved by large majorities the day they were introduced, even though members could not possibly have read the bill before casting their votes." Quick passage of the act was imperative, according to the exhortations of Attorney General Ashcroft. He threatened that if another terrorist attack occurred before the act was passed, Congress would have to answer to the American people. Most legislators responded to the pressure to pass the act quickly, although they had many misgivings. According to Republican representative Ron Paul, one of only four House members who voted against the act, "the pressure was tremendous on the members to go along and not ask too many questions."

Critics consider the far-reaching powers of the USA PATRIOT Act a dangerous threat to the civil rights of citizens, especially Arab Americans, and noncitizens, particularly from Middle Eastern countries. Democratic senator Russ
Feingold, the lone vote against the act in the Senate, explains his opposition: "I
will vote no against this bill when the roll is called. . . . Protecting the safety of
the American people is a solemn duty of the Congress. . . . But the Congress
will fulfill its duty only when it protects both the American people and the freedoms at the foundation of American society." Further, the American Civil Liberties Union (ACLU) and liberal, conservative, and libertarian groups have all
expressed concern over the potential of the act to encourage civil rights abuses.
Nadine Strossen, president of the ACLU, says that the USA PATRIOT Act puts
the rights of citizens and noncitizens alike at risk. "It's not just those who have
the misfortune or practical reality of being non-citizens or appearing to be from
certain parts of the world, but the rest of us as well. . . . The USA PATRIOT Act
has so many sweeping provisions that undermine the privacy of everybody in
this country, whether they are suspected of any crime at all, let alone terrorism."

Authors in the following chapter debate whether antiterrorist measures
threaten the civil rights of religious groups, unfairly target minorities, and jeop-
ardize the rights of immigrants. The act illustrates how difficult it is to balance
the need to prevent terrorism against the obligation to protect civil rights. Many
Americans now question if the security provided by the USA PATRIOT Act is
worth its potential to violate civil rights.

Antiterrorist Policies Jeopardize Immigrants' Civil Rights

by the Lawyers Committee for Human Rights

About the author: *The Lawyers Committee for Human Rights works in the United States and abroad to advance justice, human rights, and respect for the rule of law.*

Immediately after [the September 11, 2001, terrorist attacks on the United States] the United States' national program to admit refugees fleeing persecution around the world was shut down completely for almost three months, stranding more than 22,000 refugees who had already been told they could come to the United States. At the same time, the U.S. government began an intensive effort to apprehend accomplices and prevent another attack. Thousands of people who had nothing to do with terrorism—mostly non-citizens—were trapped in a hastily-cast net. Nearly 1,200 people were detained, mostly Arab, South Asian and Muslim men. Most of the detainees caught up in the initial investigation have now been deported. And to date, only 23,497 refugees out of 70,000 that were to have been admitted into the United States this fiscal year have arrived.

Refugee Resettlement Program Is Stopped for Three Months

For more than two decades, the United States has accepted an average of about 90,000 refugees a year to resettle here. Refugees must undergo a long application process—including interviews and security checks—to be accepted for resettlement. In the United States, church groups and other voluntary agencies meet the arriving refugees at the airport and help them to find jobs and schools. Most of them are women and children.

Refugees were already the most-scrutinized group of non-citizens coming into the United States. But after September 11, the program was shut down for nearly three months while the Administration conducted a security review. Some 22,000 refugees who had already been accepted to come to the United States—in many cases to join family members already here—were told their long-awaited trips had been canceled indefinitely. Many refugees were trapped in homeless limbo after giving up their old living quarters, unable to come to new homes or to join people who awaited them. And those stranded in Pakistan found themselves in extra danger because of anti-American sentiment there. While the program was shut down, almost no new refugees were interviewed abroad.

The refugee resettlement program formally resumed on December 11, 2001 with a flight from Zagreb [Croatia,] to Los Angeles, but this important humanitarian program is still only a faint shadow of its former self. The President [George W. Bush] signed a document authorizing 70,000 refugees to be admitted this fiscal year (ending September 30, 2002), but only 23,497 refugees have been admitted so far.

It is particularly ironic that the attacks of September 11 should have caused so much hardship to such defenseless people as refugees. As Senator Sam Brownback of Kansas said in February [2002] at a Senate hearing on the slowdown of the refugee resettlement program, "we cannot allow those events, which have already caused so much death and sorrow, to undermine our commitment to rescuing the persecuted, the widow, and the orphan."

The Post–September 11 Detainees

In the weeks and months after September 11, nearly 1,200 people, mostly Arab, South Asian and Muslim men, were detained as part of the Department of Justice investigation into the attacks. The authorities refused to disclose the identities and locations of those detained. Families, advocates, and organizations are still struggling to obtain information about those who remain in detention, as well as the many that have been deported.

Attorney General John Ashcroft characterized these arrests and detentions as an important step in the antiterrorism investigation. Speaking in October 2001, the Attorney General stated, "[O]ur anti-terrorism offensive has arrested or detained nearly 1,000 individuals as part of the September 11 terrorism investigation. Those who violated the law remain in custody. Taking suspected terrorists in violation of the law off the streets and keeping them locked up is our clear strategy to prevent terrorism within our borders."

Although the arrests and detentions were described as part of the government's "anti-terrorism offensive," few of those detained were ever charged with criminal activity tied to the investigation. The Attorney General's generic reference to the detainees as "suspected terrorists" strains credulity. Many were deported on non-criminal charges of overstaying a visa or working more hours than is permitted on a student visa. The majority of non-citizens detained by the government were long-term residents, business owners and taxpayers. Many are married to U.S. citizens and have U.S. citizen children.

Most Americans cannot recite the Bill of Rights, but all Americans are familiar with the basic principles of fairness and due process built into the U.S. Constitution including: the right not to be arbitrarily detained, and to challenge the lawfulness of detention in a court of law; the right to a speedy hearing by a competent, independent and impartial tribunal; the right to know the charges and evidence against one; and protection against torture and other cruel treatment or punishment. These constitutional principles form the foundation for international human rights treaties, drafted with U.S. leadership and support.

> *"After September 11, the [refugee resettlement] program was shut down for nearly three months while the Administration conducted a security review."*

The United States is a party to the International Covenant on Civil and Political Rights (ICCPR) which states that "No one shall be subjected to arbitrary arrest or detention." The circumstances of the government's arrests and detentions of non-citizens post–September 11 have prompted human rights advocates to submit complaints to international fora. The Human Rights Clinic at Columbia University has submitted a request to the Working Group on Arbitrary Detention of the United Nations Human Rights Commission asking that the practices of the United States, as a party to the ICCPR, be reviewed under international standards for arbitrary detention.

Preventive detention—detention prior to obtaining evidence of crime or in advance of any crime being committed—is contrary to these international principles as well as to U.S. law.

New Preventive Detention Law Is Put into Use

In announcing a new Foreign Terrorist Tracking Task Force on October 31, 2001, the Attorney General laid out an explicit strategy to exploit his previously largely unused power to detain and deport people for minor immigration status violations, as well as the power to detain those who, though not suspected of crime or immigration violations, were believed by the government to be "material witnesses" to crime. The government's theory appeared to be that, whether or not a particular person posed a threat to the United States, detention would prevent those detained from *proving* to be a threat—an "arrest and detain first, ask questions later" approach. Using the term "suspected terrorist" to refer to all those the government was detaining, the Attorney General explained that,

> We will arrest and detain any suspected terrorist who has violated the law. If suspects are found not to have links to terrorism or not to have violated the law, they'll be released. But terrorists who are in violation of the law will be convicted, in some cases be deported, and in all cases be prevented from doing further harm to Americans.

The Justice Department targeted individuals based on their gender, religion, ethnicity and national origin. In many cases, only after they were detained, were grounds sought to justify arrest and, in those cases in which immigration violations, however minor, could be identified, individuals faced lengthy detention pending deportation.

The last complete tally released by the U.S. Department of Justice in early November [2001] reported that 1182 individuals had been detained in the post-9/11 sweeps. At that point, the Department of Justice announced that it would no longer release a tally. Of that number, 752 were held on immigration charges and 129 were held on criminal charges. As of June 13, 2002, the number of immigration detainees remaining was 74 and the number of detainees held on federal criminal charges was 73. In a letter dated July 3, 2002, however, Assistant Attorney General Daniel J. Bryant stated that 81 individuals remained in detention on immigration charges and 76 on criminal charges. The discrepancies in these numbers raise questions as to their accuracy. . . .

Information about the legal basis for the detentions seeped out slowly. A small number were detained on federal criminal charges for such offenses as theft or credit card fraud, which appeared unrelated to the attacks. At least three dozen others were held as "material witnesses" on the grounds that they may have information that would be useful in a criminal or grand jury proceeding. But the great majority of detainees were held on routine immigration violations, such as overstaying a visa. . . .

Material Witnesses May Be Detained

Several detainees were held as "material witnesses"—individuals who the government alleges may have information pertaining to a criminal investigation. The law permits detention of a material witness to guarantee availability when testimony is needed in a criminal proceeding, if the government can show that the individual is a flight risk, or that the only means of obtaining testimony is detention. If the government does show a need to detain the witness, the detention should not exceed the amount of time necessary to secure the testimony by deposition.

Although material witnesses are not criminal suspects, those detained in the September 11 investigation were reportedly interrogated as if they were accused criminals and were detained in conditions that were punitive in nature. Many of these detainees were never actually required to testify in any court proceeding, and depositions were not sought to secure their testimony, raising doubts about the legitimacy of the government's assertions that they were held as material witnesses to crime.

Several of those detained under this provision challenged their detention in court. In *United States of America v. Osama Awadallah*, the use of material witness warrants to detain individuals for potential testimony before a grand jury was ruled unlawful. Awadallah is a lawful permanent resident in the United States and was held in solitary confinement in the maximum-security wing at the Metropolitan Correctional Center in New York for 20 days, based solely on a material witness warrant. The government made several misrepresentations and omissions in order to get an arrest warrant and, during the time Awadallah was imprisoned, the government failed to take steps to secure his deposition. In ordering his release, Judge Shira Scheindlin said that "since 1789, no Congress has granted the government the authority to imprison an innocent person in order to guarantee that he will testify before a grand jury conducting a criminal investigation." The government appealed the decision.

In a subsequent case in the same federal district court in New York, in *re the Application of the United States for a Material Witness Warrant*, Judge Michael Mukasey reached a different conclusion. In this case, the judge upheld the use of the material witness warrants, concluding that the government may invoke the federal material witness statute to obtain the detention of witnesses for grand jury proceedings.

Immigration Enforcement vs. Criminal Justice System

The investigation into the September 11 attacks constituted a search for criminal suspects. But the primary legal regime under which this investigation has been conducted is not the United States criminal code, but rather the immigration enforcement system. The discretion given the government under the immigration laws to arrest, detain and deport individuals is much broader than that under the nation's criminal justice system and provides fewer protections against abuse. There is little judicial oversight of the government's decision to detain an immigrant subject to deportation, even for prolonged periods. And because immigration proceedings are not considered criminal prosecutions, those detainees are not entitled to legal representation unless they can afford to retain counsel themselves.

The Administration has sought to exploit these advantages under the immigration enforcement system in order to keep people in jail for prolonged periods without access to counsel or to a judge, something it would not be entitled to do under the criminal law. Prior to September 11, individuals detained on minor immigration violations such as overstaying a visa, were routinely released on bond pending their court hearing. But since September 11, the Department of Justice has exercised its authority to prevent release on bond and to prolong detention. Of the nearly 1,200 detainees accounted for by the government, 718 were reported to have been charged with immigration violations.

> *"Although the arrests and detentions were described as part of the government's 'anti-terrorism offensive,' few of those detained were ever charged with criminal activity."*

The Department of Justice now has expanded authority that makes it easier to extend the length of detention pending deportation. This has allowed more time for the government to search for evidence on the chance that it might discover links between immigration detainees and the September 11 attacks. This strategy, while it has caused great hardship to those in detention and their families, appears to have yielded few terrorism suspects and few leads in the investigation. . . .

New Regulatory Authority

The new detention powers of the USA PATRIOT Act[1] were the most controversial provisions contained in the new law. What little debate there was in Congress about the Act centered mostly on these provisions. Although the Administration pressed hard for these expanded powers, in the more than ten months since they have had them, they have yet to use them even once. Perhaps because of the judicial review and congressional oversight amendments passed by Congress as part of the Act, the government has chosen instead to rely on regulatory authority to accomplish the same goals.

On September 17, 2001, the Attorney General issued a regulation increasing from 24 to 48 the number of hours the INS [Immigration and Naturalization Service] could detain someone without charge. In addition, the regulation authorized detention without charge for an unspecified additional "reasonable period of time" in the event of an "emergency or other extraordinary circumstance." Unlike the USA PATRIOT Act provision, this regulatory authority is not limited to detainees suspected of terrorist activity. Determining what "reasonable" means or what constitutes an "emergency" or "extraordinary circumstance" is left open to interpretation by individual INS officers. There are no meaningful checks on INS authority under this regulation.

Documents released by the INS in response to litigation under the Freedom of Information Act provide a window into the abuse that can flourish under such blanket detention authority. Of 718 so-called "special interest" detainees being held on immigration violations, 317 were held without charge for more than 48 hours. In 36 of those cases, individuals were held for 28 days or more before being charged. Thirteen people were held for more than 40 days without charge and nine were held for more than 50 days. The longest period of detention without charge was the case of a man from Saudi Arabia who was held for 119 days without charge.

These figures represent only a partial picture. According to lawyers representing a number of detainees, it is now common for the INS to fail to charge individuals within the prescribed 48 hours. The bipartisan effort in Congress to include in the USA PATRIOT Act a seven-day charge requirement to curb abuse of new government powers has been completely ineffectual. Current practice under INS regulations involves detention without charge not only for a week, but for months.

1. The USA PATRIOT Act was passed on October 26, 2001, and grants broad powers to the Attorney General to detain noncitizens suspected of terrorist activities.

Detention Powers Were Expanded

Another regulation providing expanded detention powers to the INS, which took effect on October 29, 2001, gives the Executive Office for Immigration Review expanded authority to suspend, at the request of the INS, an immigration judge's decision that a detainee should be released on bond. Prior to this Rule, once an alien was ordered released on bond by an immigration judge, the INS could request a stay only in limited circumstances involving aliens subject to mandatory detention, such as those convicted of certain aggravated felonies. The new regulation expands this authority to include any case where an alien has been detained while removal proceedings were pending or where bond has been set at $10,000 or more. Under these regulations, an INS trial attorney (the prosecutor in immigration proceedings) is authorized, in effect, to overrule the judge's order that a detainee be released. There is no requirement that the individual be suspected of a crime or terrorist activity. As the appeal process is lengthy, and bond in post-September 11 cases has routinely been high, the result has been prolonged periods of detention.

The automatic stay rule was recently declared a violation of due process by a district court judge in the case of *Almonte-Vargas v. Kenneth Elwood.* Judge R. Barclay Surrick stated in his decision that due process is not satisfied where an individualized custody determination is "effectively a charade."

> *"A detainee is presumed guilty until proven innocent."*

Detainees otherwise eligible for release on bond were regularly denied parole based on an obscure declaration by the government that they had not received "clearance," a process that has still not been explained. It appears that "clearance" is what is granted when the authorities have ruled out the possibility of any connection between the detainee and terrorist activity. Records on the operation of this procedure are unavailable to the public or the courts. This practice turns the presumption of innocence on its head. Essentially, a detainee is presumed guilty until proven innocent.

Access to Counsel Was Made More Difficult

Although not entitled to court-appointed counsel, immigration detainees are entitled to have access to counsel at their own expense. In ordinary times, the immigration system is nearly impossible to navigate without a lawyer. But since September 11, with the government's panoply of new powers and commitment to aggressive enforcement, detainees are particularly disadvantaged if they are without legal representation. Obviously, detention impedes the ability to access counsel, but INS rules require that detainees be informed of their right to counsel and about resources available for pro bono representation; provided with access to telephones free of charge for legal calls; and provided appropriate time for visits from their attorney.

After September 11, however, immigration detainees have faced greater obstacles to accessing legal representation, including: very limited access to telephones (detainees in Passaic County Jail were allowed only one phone call to an attorney per week) and in some instances collect calling only; outdated phone lists for legal service organizations; failure to provide detainees with the handbooks that contain the information they need to find counsel; and restrictions on lawyers trying to gain access to clients or prospective clients.

In addition to these practical obstacles to effective access to counsel, the Attorney General has issued a new directive authorizing the government to listen in on attorney-client conversations in situations where it suspects the communication may facilitate criminal acts. The government already had the authority to do this, but that power was tempered by a requirement that it first make a showing to a judge that such monitoring was necessary. Now, the executive branch has the power to unilaterally make such decisions, without oversight by the judiciary. The new rule requires the government to notify attorneys and their clients in advance when monitoring will occur, making it unlikely that the government will gain any useful information about terrorist plots. But the rule is likely to significantly disrupt attorney-client communications, and infringe on what the Supreme Court has described as "the oldest of the privileges for confidential communications known to the common law," designed "to encourage full and frank communication between attorneys and their clients and thereby promote broader public interests in the observance of law and administration of justice."

The Names of Detainees Have Been Kept Secret

The government has sought to keep secret the names of the people it has in detention and the charges, if any, on which they are being held. Various rationales have been offered in defense of this policy, ranging from concern for the privacy of the detainees to fear that releasing information about who the government has in custody would tip off the terrorist network about U.S. investigative strategy. But many sectors of the public, including the media, public interest groups, and members of Congress, have sought access to this information.

The ACLU [American Civil Liberties Union] filed a lawsuit seeking release of the names of detainees being held at two county jails in New Jersey, under a state law which "stipulates that the names and the dates of entry of all inmates in county jails, without exception, 'shall be open to public inspection.' New Jersey Superior Court Judge Arthur D'Italia ruled against the government, calling secret detentions "odious to a democratic society." In response to the ruling, the Department of Justice issued a new regulation prohibiting state authorities from releasing information about immigration detainees. The state court ruling ordering release of the information was effectively overruled by the Justice Department.

At the federal level, a coalition of organizations led by the Center for National Security Studies filed suit in federal district court in the District of Columbia against the Department of Justice to seek responses to their request for information about the detainees under the Freedom of Information Act.

Holding that "[s]ecret arrests are profoundly antithetical to the bedrock values that characterize a free and open [society] such as ours," and noting that none of the detainees held on immigration charges had been tied to terrorism, Judge Gladys Kessler ordered the government to release the names of detainees and their lawyers. "The first priority of the judicial branch must be to ensure that our government always operates within the statutory and constitutional constraints which distinguish a democracy from a dictatorship," Judge Kessler said. The Justice Department refused to comply and appealed the decision.

In addition to withholding the names of detainees, the Attorney General has also asserted the power to close immigration hearings to the public, including to families of the detainees, in cases of "special interest" to the government. The government has not revealed the criteria by which it classifies a case being of "special interest." Instructions on how to comply with the Attorney General's order that certain hearings be held in secret are contained in a September 21, 2001 memorandum issued by Chief Immigration Judge Michael J. Creppy. The internal memorandum instructs immigration judges to: paper over windows in their courtrooms; deny access to visitors, family and the press; remove cases from the docket list; and change computerized docket systems to ensure that case names and other information do not appear in any publicly accessible format. . . .

> *"A government operating in the shadow of secrecy stands in complete opposition to the society envisioned by the Framers of our Constitution."*

When the Justice Department designated the case of Rabih Haddad, a well-known Muslim cleric in Michigan, as a "special interest" case and closed his immigration proceedings to the public, Representative John Conyers (D-MI), the ACLU and the Detroit Free Press joined other members of the public in challenging the government's policy of closed hearings. Federal District Judge Nancy G. Edmunds ruled that blanket closure of deportation hearings was unconstitutional. . . .

Undeterred by adverse rulings in federal court, the Department of Justice issued a new regulation attempting to ensure its ability to hold secret hearings. Under the new measure, immigration judges are directed to grant "protective orders" on a case-by-case basis to bar disclosure of information which the government wants kept secret. The regulation seeks to replicate the effect of the Creppy memorandum, while addressing the concerns reflected in court decisions about a lack of case-by-case determinations of risk.

"Blanket Closures" Are Unconstitutional

The government also sought to preserve its power to close all "special interest" cases by appealing its loss in the Rabih Haddad case to the U.S. Court of Appeals for the Sixth Circuit. But on August 26, 2002, the Sixth Circuit affirmed the lower court's ruling and held "the blanket closure of deportation hearings in 'special interest' cases unconstitutional." Judge Damon J. Keith, who wrote the opinion, stated that, by asserting "national security" concerns,

> the Government seeks a process where it may, without review, designate certain classes of cases as "special interest cases" and, behind closed doors, adjudicate the merits of these cases to deprive non-citizens of their fundamental liberty interests. . . . This, we simply may not countenance. A government operating in the shadow of secrecy stands in complete opposition to the society envisioned by the Framers of our Constitution.

Using Military Tribunals to Try Suspected Terrorists Is Not Justified

by the *St. Louis Post-Dispatch*

About the author: *The* St. Louis Post-Dispatch *is a daily newspaper.*

President George W. Bush's plan to use military tribunals to try terrorist suspects is founded on three flawed assumptions: that military trials can be fair in the United States even if they aren't fair in other countries; that U.S. military tribunals provide the same kind of legal protections as courts-martial; and that historical precedents justify transplanting 19th century notions of fairness into the 21st century.

The claim that U.S. military tribunals will be fair is too self-serving to be credible. For years, the United States has excoriated dozens of countries—Peru, Russia, China and Sudan among others—for unfair military trials. Mr. Bush argues that our military courts will be different. That borders on a double standard.

History Does Not Justify Tribunals

Mr. Bush's order providing for military tribunals already has the hallmarks of unfairness: All or part of the trial could be closed. Military officers replace impartial judges and juries. Most rules of evidence are tossed out as is the requirement for proof beyond a reasonable doubt. The suspect doesn't have the right to choose a lawyer. Conviction and execution require only a two-thirds vote. Appeals to federal court are barred, effectively suspending the writ of habeas corpus.

The absence of those basic protections also refutes the White House claim that military tribunals provide terrorists with the same protections Americans receive in courts-martial. In fact, courts-martial have jury trials, appeals and unanimous verdicts. Little wonder, then, that Spain balked at turning over al-Qaida members it arrested.

Mr. Bush maintains that the tribunals could provide a safer, more efficient way of prosecuting a group of al-Qaida members captured in Afghanistan. That narrow use might not be objectionable. But Mr. Bush's order also permits the use of the tribunals to try some of the immigrants detained in the United States.

The weakest of the Bush assumptions is that history justifies the tribunals. But a careful reading of U.S. history leads to the conclusion that military tribunals should not be used when the civil courts are available.

Civil War and World War II

The White House rests its dubious defense of tribunals on World War II and the Civil War. Both episodes were dark chapters in American history, in which justice was sacrificed to presidential power. President Abraham Lincoln suspended the writ of habeas corpus—a protection against false imprisonment—during the first year of the Civil War; he ignored the chief justice who told him he could not.

In 1864, Lambdin P. Milligan, an Indiana politician, was tried before a military commission for conspiracy to release Confederate prisoners. The evidence showed that Mr. Milligan was a member of the Sons of Liberty, but little else. After the war, Justice David Davis said the president could not try Mr. Milligan or any other civilian before a military commission when the civil courts were open for business. In a famous passage—relevant today—Mr. Davis wrote: "The Constitution of the United States is a law for rulers and people, equally in war and in peace, and covers with the shield of its protection all classes of men, at all times and under all circumstances."

The most recent use of military tribunals was Franklin Roosevelt's prosecution of eight saboteurs who sneaked into the country on German submarines in 1942. One of the spies, an American citizen, tipped off the FBI, but J. Edgar Hoover boasted that he had cracked the case. Historians concluded that Mr. Roosevelt wanted a secret military trial to avoid the embarrassing revelation that Mr. Hoover had little to do with solving the crime. The seven Army major generals who heard the evidence were often confused by the law and standards of evidence. When the lawyer for the men appealed to the Supreme Court, Mr. Roosevelt's attorney general told the justices privately that the president would hang the Germans no matter what the court did. The court quickly upheld the convictions, releasing its opinion after six of the eight had been executed. That same year, the court upheld the detention of 100,000 Japanese-Americans.

"Bring the terrorists to justice . . . provide them with a trial that is . . . fair in reality and . . . looks fair in the eyes of the world."

At least Mr. Roosevelt had the approval of Congress for his tribunals. Mr. Bush does not. He insists that his war power gives him the authority to set up tribunals on his own. The Supreme Court usually defers to the president in wartime and probably would again. But when the court invalidated President Harry S Truman's seizure of the steel mills during the Korean war, it said that a president acts in a "zone of twilight" when he doesn't have Congress' acquiescence.

The U.S. goal in the upcoming prosecutions is straightforward: Bring the terrorists to justice and provide them with a trial that is both fair in reality and that looks fair in the eyes of the world.

The best road to that goal would be creating an international court, like the one at The Hague. Second best is trial in federal court. Attorney General John D. Ashcroft fears "Osama TV." Granted, big trials can be media circuses. But Mr. Ashcroft sells short our system of justice. No judge is going to permit a televised trial, O.J. Simpson–style. The most self-defeating approach is a closed military tribunal. Even if it looks fair to us, it is going to look like a kangaroo court to the rest of the world.

Antiterrorist Efforts Unfairly Target Arab Americans

by Tseming Yang

About the author: *Tseming Yang is an associate professor of law at Vermont Law School.*

In the wake of the Sept. 11 [2001] terrorist attacks, Supreme Court Justice Sandra Day O'Connor declared, "We're likely to experience more restrictions on our personal freedoms than has ever been the case in our country."

Unfortunately, her collective statement regarding "our" personal freedoms perpetuates a myth. The reality is that only a minority will truly bear the burden of restricted liberties. We must come to grips with this truth, since new anti-terrorism legislation will be signed into law shortly.[1]

The barbaric acts of terrorism have understandably led to increased police and military activities, both to prevent future violence and to find the parties responsible for the attacks. These measures may well impact "all of us," either through the inconvenience of delays or by decreased privacy. Yet the reality is that Arab-Americans, Muslims and those who look like them are the ones who will be most affected by the government's actions.

The war on terrorism will not affect all citizens equally. Some are simply more vulnerable to its effects than others. For example, times of crisis magnify the suspicions and unconscious biases to which minority groups are already subject. This was made painfully obvious during World War II, when thousands of American citizens and permanent residents of Japanese ancestry were interned, though they had nothing to do with Japan's attacks on Pearl Harbor.

President [George W.] Bush and the Congress have publicly denounced stereotyping and revenge against today's "suspect" groups. However, the actions of law enforcement, airlines and the media which focus attention and sus-

1. The USA PATRIOT Act became law on October 26, 2001.

picions on Arab-Americans and Muslims speak louder than such pronounce-ments. In fact, some provisions of the pending anti-terrorism bill, which would allow for extended detention of immigrants beyond that permitted for citizens, sends that same message of suspicion.

More insidiously, for those who already hold stereotypical beliefs about people of other races generally, and fears about Arab-Americans and Muslims as potential terrorists specifically, these official actions only serve to le-gitimize their fears and suspicions. Those who are truly racially preju-diced may feel emboldened to act upon those prejudices.

> *"The reality is that Arab-Americans, Muslims and those who look like them are the ones who will be most affected by the governments's actions."*

Since Sept. 11, numerous acts of hate and vengeance, including assaults, vio-lent threats and vandalism have targeted Arab-Americans, Muslims and South Asians, in particular Sikhs. In Michigan, an Arab-American was dragged out of bed, shot 12 times, and killed by an assailant who vowed vengeance for the ter-rorist attacks. In Arizona, a Sikh gas station owner was shot and killed. The acts of hatred against Sikhs are particularly ironic because most Sikhs are Indian and, as a religious group, are unaffiliated with Islam.

Minorities Must Be Protected

These incidents make clear that the victims of the terrorist attacks include not only those who were directly killed or injured on Sept. 11, but indirectly the overwhelming majority of Muslims and Arab-Americans as well. While they have had nothing to do with the terrorists, they nevertheless have become scapegoats.

Minorities need the greatest legal protections during times of crisis, but the judicial response has been inadequate. The United States Supreme Court has never overturned its cases that found the wartime internment of Japanese-Americans to be legal, and Chief Justice William Rehnquist has indicated that if faced again with a Pearl Harbor-type crisis, the court might sanction those very same wartime measures anew.

How little the Supreme Court might offer to minorities was driven home a few weeks ago, when the court refused to review a case involving allegations of racial profiling in Oneonta, N.Y., after police there had rounded up dozens of black men while searching for a rape suspect.

Most Americans agree that anger over the terrorist attacks cannot justify retal-iation against those who are connected to the alleged perpetrators only by mem-bership in the Islamic religion, Arab ancestry or similar physical appearance, nor can it serve as an excuse for racial bigotry and hatred. Yet we cannot fully act on such convictions until we see past the myth that anti-terrorism measures will affect us all to the same degree.

The anti-terrorism legislation has already been modified much to address civil liberties concerns. However, its consequences will fall most harshly on minority groups and immigrants who are already the subject of biases and prejudices. We should not kid ourselves about that. This makes it doubly important for each of us to speak out when we see anger turn into vengeance and scapegoating, and when prejudice parades around as false patriotism and legalized suspicion.

In the end, the law and the courts cannot save us from our own racial and religious biases and prejudices—only we can.

Antiterrorist Policies Do Not Jeopardize Immigrants' Civil Rights

by Mark Krikorian

About the author: *Mark Krikorian is the executive director of the Center for Immigration Studies, a think tank devoted exclusively to research and policy analysis of the economic, social, demographic, fiscal, and other impacts of immigration on the United States.*

> *"Immigration is not a right guaranteed by the U.S. Constitution to everyone and anyone in the world who wishes to come to the United States. It is a privilege granted by the people of the United States to those whom we choose to admit."* —Barbara Jordan, August 12, 1995

Thank you for the opportunity to participate in this briefing on immigration and civil rights in the wake of the September 11 [2001] jihadist atrocities. We are faced with two questions relating to civil liberties: First, Is immigration a civil right? And second, What is the best way to create an environment respectful of immigrants living among us?

Immigration Is Not a Civil Right

Article I, Section 8, Clause 4 of the Constitution grants Congress the power to establish a "uniform Rule of Naturalization." From this has developed the "plenary power doctrine," which holds that Congress has complete authority over immigration matters. The Supreme Court has said that "over no conceivable subject" is federal power greater than it is over immigration. As a consequence, as the Court has said elsewhere, "In the exercise of its broad power over naturalization and immigration, Congress regularly makes rules that would be unacceptable if applied to citizens."

This is as it should be, since control over immigration is fundamental to na-

Mark Kirkorian, testimony before the U.S. Commission of Civil Rights, Washington, DC, October 12, 2001.

tional sovereignty. If "We the People of the United States" have ordained and established the Constitution, then we by definition retain the power to determine who is, and is not, a member of the American people. Thus, the decision to admit or exclude foreign citizens is a matter solely in the hands of the elected representatives of the people, and any one from abroad who is admitted to travel or live among us does so as a guest, remaining here at our pleasure, until such time as we agree to permit him to become a member of our people. In effect, foreign citizens, even if they are here illegally, enjoy the human rights endowed to them by God, but they remain here at our discretion and the specifics of their due process rights are determined by Congress.

This is relevant in assessing many of the measures to tighten immigration control recommended in the wake of the September 11 attacks. All 19 hijackers were, after all, foreign citizens, as are many of those detained as possible accomplices or witnesses. This was also the case with the conspirators in the first World Trade Center attack, the 1993 CIA assassinations, and the foiled bomb plots in New York in 1995 and in Washington state in 1999. Foreign citizens, or naturalized immigrants, are almost certain to be responsible for the next attack, whether it comes in the next few days, as the FBI has warned, or farther in the future.

To begin at the first step in the process of coming to the United States, there is likely to be special scrutiny applied to visa applicants from Muslim countries and even to people of Middle Eastern birth who now hold other citizenship. Whether or not ethnic or religious profiling is an appropriate tool in the government's dealings with American citizens, there are no civil rights implications of such profiling of foreign citizens overseas. The United States government may refuse entry to any foreign citizen, for any reason, at any time. It is precisely to preserve this irreducible element of national sovereignty that repeated attempts to subject visa refusals to review have been rebuffed by Congress.

One of the grounds for exclusion may well be expanded as a result of the jihadist attacks, one that would not be unacceptable if applied to citizens but clearly permitted, indeed mandated, when applied to non-citizens abroad. Current law makes it extremely difficult to turn down a visa applicant because of his "beliefs, statements, or associations, if such beliefs, statements, or associations would be lawful within the United States." To keep out a terrorist sympathizer, who publicly cheers the murder of Americans but who, as far as we know, hasn't yet raised money for terrorist groups or

> *"Foreign citizens . . . remain here at our discretion and the specifics of their due process rights are determined by Congress."*

planned out their assaults, the Secretary of State must personally make the decision and then report each individual instance to four congressional committees. It is imperative that visa officers be given a freer hand in excluding enemies of

America, even if their hatred for us would be constitutionally protected if articulated by citizens. The First Amendment does not apply to foreigners abroad.

"Expedited Exclusion" Seeks to End Asylum Abuses

Fingerprinting of visa applicants is another change likely in the wake of the attacks. Ideally, foreign visitors and students and workers would have their fingerprints digitally scanned when applying for their visas, scanned again when entering the country, and again upon departure. Again, despite claims to the contrary, there are no civil rights implications of this security measure; this would simply be one of the conditions of being a guest in the United States.

The next stage in coming to the United States is at the border. Here, a tool to prevent the penetration of our system by terrorists and others has already been implemented. Although many have claimed that there are civil rights consequences to the procedure known as "expedited exclusion," enacted in the 1996 immigration law, there are no such consequences. That provision sought to end asylum abuses through the expedited exclusion of false asylum claimants at airports; when a person who has arrived in the United States with no documents or forged documents claims asylum, the initial plausibility of his claim may be judged by the immigration officer, to be reviewed by his supervisor if the officer makes a negative determination, and the alien may then be prevented from entering the United States and pursuing an asylum claim.

> *"Foreign citizens, or naturalized immigrants, are almost certain to be responsible for the next [terrorist] attack."*

Again, this is part of Congress's plenary power over immigration and there are no civil rights consequences of this policy.

And, finally, within the country, non-citizens do have rights, more if they are permanent residents, and thus candidate-members of the American people, and fewer if they are "nonimmigrants," i.e., on some sort of temporary visa. One change in the treatment of non-immigrants that is almost certain to be implemented in the wake of September 11 is the tracking of foreign students. Under a pilot program mandated by the 1996 immigration law, about two dozen colleges are participating in a program that requires the schools to update the INS [Immigration and Naturalization Service] on a quarterly basis about the academic status, address, field of study, etc. of all foreign students. This program was set to expand to all schools accepting foreign students over the next several years, but will now be sped up. Many foreign students and university spokesmen have complained about this as "unfair" or "discriminatory," using civil rights language to express their displeasure. But of course, as I have discussed, these students are here purely as guests in our house, and we are entitled to place whatever conditions we deem appropriate on their stay.

The same is true regarding the registration of lawful permanent residents. In

1940, as a security measure to try to prevent our enemies from infiltrating spies and saboteurs in immigrant communities, Congress required registration of all legal immigrants, which included a requirement that each alien notify the INS annually of his whereabouts. This notification requirement was discontinued in 1981, and shouldn't be revived in that form—members of terrorist sleeper cells cannot be expected to dutifully send in their addresses. However, a computerized system to verify the employment eligibility of new hires (pilots for which were mandated by the 1996 immigration law) could be a very effective tool in tracking the whereabouts of non-citizen legal immigrants and would, in effect, serve as a registration program for most resident aliens.

> *"The United States government may refuse entry to any foreign citizen, for any reason, at any time."*

Deportation Is Not Punishment

Deportation policy is another area where some have warned that measures recently passed or now proposed would have civil rights implications. The problem with this view is that deportation is not punishment—only non-citizens may be deported, and they are either here as our guests or as illegal aliens, and may be removed at any time so long as lawful procedures are followed. In the Supreme Court's 1999 ruling in *Reno v. American-Arab Anti-Discrimination Committee*, for instance, the free speech rights of, in this case, illegal aliens were sharply, and appropriately limited in the context of deportation proceedings. In the wake of September 11, it is possible that further limitations on speech and affiliation will be imposed on non-citizens, entirely appropriate limitations in such a national emergency.

The 1996 anti-terrorism and immigration laws also allowed the use of classified evidence in deportation proceedings of suspected terrorists. Virtually all of the tiny number of cases using secret evidence have involved Arabs and/or Muslims, a result which has given rise to civil rights complaints. There has even been legislation to require that such classified evidence be disclosed, which would compromise intelligence sources and methods. Though little has been heard about this since September 11, complaints based on civil rights concerns will eventually resurface. Again, deportation is not punishment—immigration proceedings are administrative, not criminal, and their purpose, according to the Supreme Court, is to "provide a streamlined determination of eligibility to remain in this country, nothing more." Thus, as the FBI general counsel noted in testimony last year, "the full range of rights guaranteed a criminal defendant, including the Sixth Amendment's right to confrontation of evidence, are not applicable in immigration proceedings."

Even the deportation provision in the original version of the administration's anti-terrorism package would not have had any civil rights consequences. That provision, since dropped, would have allowed deportation of persons certified as having terrorist ties without the presentation of any evidence at all. This is admittedly an emergency measure, but it would have been entirely appropriate, and may yet be implemented, as further terrorist attacks take place. Any ability accorded the alien to appeal deportation decisions is an act of grace on the part of the American people, rather than a right possessed by the alien. The courts thus have a role in ensuring that the alien is accorded due process of law, but the content of the law regarding removal of aliens is not a proper object of constitutional review.

It would be unfortunate if, in our effort to prevent another 6,000 American deaths—or 60,000 or 600,000—we were inadvertently to deport some foreign citizens who pose no threat to us. But their presence here is a privilege we grant, not a right they have exercised, and we may withdraw that privilege for any reason.

Indefinite Detention Is Unacceptable

Detention is another matter. Although INS rules allowing longer detention for illegal aliens before instituting proceedings are simple common sense, indefinite denial of liberty is disturbing, as the Supreme Court concluded in the *Zadvyas v. Davis* case. Even non-citizens possess the natural rights of life, liberty, and property, and the situation of those colloquially called "lifers"—reportable aliens whose countries of citizenship will not accept them back—is untenable. Only those deemed by the INS to be a threat to others should be kept in detention, while the federal government should seek political solutions to coerce, if necessary, the sending countries to take back their criminal citizens. There are some instances, however, where this simply won't happen, since the people finding themselves in this situation are almost always refugees fleeing communist or other despotic regimes hostile to the United States.

Given that coming to America is a privilege and not a right, we still should seek to create a climate welcoming to those immigrants we do admit. In other words, although we have the right, and the duty, to regulate immigration to the benefit of the American people, it is desirable as a policy matter that the climate we create for immigrants is as welcoming as possible. How may we accomplish this?

> *"It is possible that further limitations on speech and affiliation will be imposed on non-citizens, entirely appropriate limitations in such a national emergency."*

The United States admits between 700,000 and 900,000 legal immigrants per year, plus millions of long-term and short-term visitors (tourists, business travelers, students, workers, et al.). What's more, it is much easier for immigrants to become citizens in our country than in virtually any other—[in 2002] alone, almost 900,000 people began the year as foreigners and ended it as Americans.

The result is that today there are about 31 million foreign-born people in the United States, more than 60 percent of them non-citizens. This is the largest wave of immigration in the nation's history, surpassing the period at the turn of the last century, and with no end in sight. This high level of immigration has a variety of economic, fiscal, social, demographic, and political costs and benefits, which are not appropriate subjects for this briefing. But it is appropriate to ask how this unprecedented flow of newcomers affects the treatment of immigrants and the nature of their welcome.

Unfortunately, there is an inverse relationship between the level of immigration and the hospitality accorded newcomers. In other words, more immigration results in harsher treatment for the immigrants. We have seen this process over the past generation as immigration has steadily increased in tandem with restrictions on immigrants. Political responses to this increasing immigration began in 1994 with the overwhelming passage by Californians of Proposition 187, which sought to deny certain government services to illegal aliens, and continued through 1996, with the passage of laws aimed at terrorism, immigration, and welfare. Although all of these changes were within our power as a people to make and raise no legitimate constitutional concerns, some were unfortunately anti-immigrant, such as the sweeping welfare eligibility bans for legal immigrants or the retroactivity of the expanded definition of deportable offenses. Even the many elements of those laws which were positive were made necessary by high immigration—such as expedited exclusion or the rules making immigrant sponsorship agreements legally enforceable.

Give Fewer Immigrants a Warmer Welcome

This contradiction is not merely a function of ethnic animus or fear of the other, though I have no doubt they play a role. Even in the absence of our darker impulses, mass immigration necessitates more restrictive treatment of immigrants. For instance, the presence of a large and continually increasing number of poor people forces us to set priorities regarding social spending, whereas a small number of immigrants, even if they made relatively heavy use of welfare, would not force such choices. Also, the rapid population growth driven mainly by high immigration fuels the growth in government regulation of all aspects of life, whereas lower population density necessitates less government regulation of society. More immigration also means more immigrant criminals, whatever the general crime rate among immigrants, and this requires more restrictive rules governing non-citizen criminals, whereas a lower level of immigration would not give rise to the need for such special rules.

Therefore, we cannot have pro-immigrant policy of high immigration, however much many on the left seek it. What we have now is an anti-immigrant policy of high immigration, crafted mainly by the libertarian wing of the Republican Party, and especially by Spencer Abraham, formerly a senator and now Secretary of Energy.

There are two other policy options: One is an anti-immigrant policy of low immigration. There are people who actually support this, but their number is small and their political impact is infinitesimal. The other option is a pro-immigrant policy of low immigration, one that admits fewer immigrants but extends a warmer welcome to those who are admitted. This is the only way in the real world to cultivate a pro-immigrant policy that would defuse many of the civil rights concerns, valid or not, surrounding our treatment of non-citizens.

Using Military Tribunals to Try Suspected Terrorists Is Justified

by Bruce Tucker Smith

About the author: *Bruce Tucker Smith is a U.S. administrative-law judge and serves as a reservist in the Air Force Judge Advocate General's Department.*

The United States is at war and, in these extraordinary times, the law must be wielded not as a shield but as a sword. The legal response to the terrorist attacks must be an integral part of, not distinct from, America's war effort. Tribunals will be swift, certain and fair. They will provide basic due process and will vindicate an aggrieved nation. Above all, the tribunals will render justice quickly: Justice delayed is most assuredly justice denied.

Unaccustomed as we are to hearing a president speak as a wartime commander in chief, ours has done so, declaring that a national emergency warrants activation of military tribunals to hear the prosecutions of those persons who wrought our latest day of infamy. Those noncitizen terror warriors who will stand before the tribunals are not entitled to the full protections of a system they most certainly would have destroyed.

Two Definitions of Terrorism

The United States assuredly is at war in the factual sense but not precisely in the legal sense. That uncertainty poses a dilemma: What to do with a terror warrior once he is run to ground, for he is neither a lawful combatant nor a criminal in the classic sense. Military tribunals seem a highly appropriate forum in which to resolve the interwoven legal, factual and political issues raised in this new war by and against terrorism.

Legally speaking, the definition of terrorism lies somewhere in the murky half-light between war and crime. Either appellation fits, but neither suits. Admittedly, this is not a congressionally declared war between "states," because neither al-Qaeda nor the Taliban is a recognizable "state." They neither govern, at least in the classic sense, a defined territory nor engage in formal international relations with other "states." Thus, it might be overreaching to call their actions "war crimes."

Conversely the heinous acts of September 11 (together with prior, related attacks on the USS *Cole*, Khobar Towers, etc.) are more than a series of ordinary criminal actions by independent actors. There is certainly an odor of highly coordinated state sponsorship behind the villainy.

The unclear legal nature of this new war dictates that neither domestic criminal courts, military courts-martial nor international courts are appropriate prosecutorial venues.

> *"Tribunals will be swift, certain and fair."*

Trials in civilian criminal courts would marginalize the importance of those prosecutions. The September 11 attacks transcend common criminality because terrorism of this magnitude is a political statement and an assault against American society itself. When terrorists targeted U.S. citizens on such a massive scale, they violated even the legitimate acts of war under international law.

Sadly, in the last decade we failed to recognize terror warriors for what they were. We regarded them as ordinary criminals and afforded them all the constitutional protections our criminal-justice system provides. Witness the two federal prosecutions resulting from the 1993 World Trade Center bombing. The first trial lasted more than five months, suffered a parade of more than 200 witnesses and endured the presentation of more than a thousand exhibits. The second trial was nearly eight months long and saw as many witnesses and nearly as much evidence. Of greater importance, a message was lost on the nation at large: Had the United States prosecuted those terrorists before military tribunals, Americans might have been awakened to a pre-existing and ongoing state of war that finally was brought into specific relief on September 11.

Military Tribunals Are the Best Solution

Civilian courts insist upon unanimity among 12 jurors to sustain a criminal conviction. That tradition is rooted in the premise that we would rather free the guilty than condemn the innocent. But when the very real probability exists that terrorists (who are not U.S. citizens and who may be in this country illegally) likely will inflict mass murder and property damage anew, the niceties of traditional due process become untenable. The scale of the terrorist attacks has been too great; the perspective of civilian courts too narrow. The probability of time-consuming "loopholery" and attorney grandstanding are certain; the promise of a media-driven spectacle is a given. Open-air civilian courts simply are the wrong place to prosecute terror warriors.

Trial by military courts-martial is equally inappropriate because, generally speaking, military courts-martial provide more procedural due process to the accused than do most civilian courts and certainly far more than terrorists deserve. The people of the United States certainly will ask why the United States would afford the same legal protections to terrorists as it guarantees those U.S. servicemembers who defend the nation.

A third option, trial before an international court (such as those hearing Serbian and Rwandan war-crimes prosecutions), is inappropriate because the United States would have virtually no control over either the proceedings or the punishments. The greatest risk, of course, is that other national political agendas would work their way into the spotlight, and any given trial could turn into a referendum on U.S. foreign policy.

The best solution, trials before military tribunals, will ensure that the dictates of both fundamental fairness and national security are quickly met.

Military Tribunals Have Historical Precedent

There is nothing legally inappropriate nor historically inconsistent about the reactivated tribunals. Presidents Abraham Lincoln and Franklin D. Roosevelt made extensive use of tribunals during the Civil War and World War II, respectively, and the Supreme Court has twice affirmed the constitutionality of the tribunals. In *Ex Parte Quirin*, 317 U.S. 1 (1942), the court noted, "The . . . enemy combatants who without uniform come secretly through the lines for the purpose of waging war by destruction of life or property, are . . . offenders against the law of war subject to trial and punishment by military Tribunals." And, in *Re: Yamashita*, 327 U.S. 1 (1946), the court said military tribunals are not bound by the dictates of due process as we are in our everyday civilian courts. It is noteworthy, however, that tribunals employed during World War II acquitted some German and Japanese defendants.

Criticism that the tribunals do not afford potential defendants enough procedural protection is ironic for, in reality, terrorists are entitled to no due-process rights whatsoever. International law says that only "lawful" enemy combatants are entitled to due process, established by proof that those combatants fight under a clearly designated flag or symbol visible at a distance; serve in a military force under a recognized chain of command; carry arms openly to establish combatant status clearly; and engage in operations in accord with the established laws of war.

> *"There is nothing legally inappropriate nor historically inconsistent about the . . . tribunals."*

It is doubtful that the al-Qaeda terrorists qualify as lawful combatants. Hence, the procedural rights identified in the president's order—or any procedures at present being crafted by attorneys for the departments of Defense and Justice—are far more than the al-Qaeda terror warriors legally are entitled to receive.

It was never thinkable that even terrorists would be denied fair process. That is why the commander in chief's order specifically affirms due process and carefully directs that only noncitizens will stand before the tribunals. The order does not contemplate the prosecution of U.S. citizens or even enemy soldiers who obey the laws of armed conflict. Anyone arrested, detained or tried in the United States by a tribunal will be able to challenge the tribunal's jurisdiction through a writ of habeas corpus in an appropriate federal court. Moreover, tribunal hearings will be "full and fair." Every person tried before a tribunal will be informed of the charges against him, be represented by qualified counsel and be allowed to present a defense. The order also ensures judicial review by civilian courts.

Tribunals will not be trials by traditional military courts-martial; the rules will be entirely different. Yet, the subtext of the criticism leveled against the tribunals is that a defendant cannot get a fair trial; that somehow, a trial by military judges and prosecutors would be a sham. Such criticism is utterly without merit and horribly uninformed. Tribunals will be designed, prosecuted, defended and adjudicated by the best attorneys in uniform—counselors at law who have been educated at U.S. law schools and who have been steeped in a tradition of respect for the due-process rights of the accused.

During my nearly two decades of service as both a military prosecutor and defense counsel, it has been demonstrated repeatedly to me that those men and women practicing within our U.S. military-justice system simply are the finest such practitioners in the world. Unlike their civilian counterparts, military lawyers are governed by appellate case law, which actually forbids unlawful political or command influence over proceedings, ensures vigorous defense advocacy by competent counsel and insists upon procedural fairness. This is the rich cultural and legal soil from which the participants in the tribunals have grown.

Tribunals Are Necessary

Tribunals are the best solution because civilian jurors and judges won't have to face personal risks that may be attendant to terrorist trials. Tribunals allow the government to use classified information as evidence without compromising either national security or the lives of Americans on the front lines of battle. Tribunals will dispense justice swiftly and fairly, without unnecessary pretrial proceedings or lengthy post-trial appeals, lest other terrorists become emboldened by the slow grind of our criminal-justice system.

Whether trying terrorists by tribunal will lower the United States in the esteem of the world community is utterly irrelevant. Those who have admired the United States will continue to do so; those who revile us will not change their minds simply because we offered the full panoply of procedural due process to terrorists.

Our focus must remain constant and vigilant: We are at war and we must free ourselves of the notion that the September 11 terror attacks merely were crimes to be resolved in our often tediously slow criminal courts. We must appreciate that the tribunals are a necessary part of the war effort.

The tribunals are a sword that must be wielded with speed, but most certainly with due care.

Antiterrorism Efforts Targeting Arab Americans Are Justified

by Heather MacDonald

About the author: *Heather MacDonald is a contributing editor to* City Journal, *a conservative New York City publication, and the author of* Are Cops Racist?

I've been amusing myself recently with the following experiment: I call up the most strident anti-police activists of recent years, including Washington's local police scourge, Georgetown law professor David Cole, who argues that every aspect of the criminal justice system is racist. I ask these police critics the following question: Suppose that in the wake of [the September 11, 2001, terrorist attacks on America] the FBI decides to check out recent graduates of American flight schools to see who else may be plotting to use airplanes as weapons. Which students, I ask, should the FBI investigate—all of the would-be pilots, or a subset of them?

Without exception, I get the following answer: "The FBI should investigate everyone."

"Everyone?" I respond. "That's a big number. You'd be stretching the resources of the FBI dangerously thin. Wouldn't you look," I ask, "at a student from Saudi Arabia more closely than you would at someone from Kentucky?"

Nope, comes the reply. The FBI has to investigate everyone equally to avoid racism. A civil liberties law professor from St. Louis University even insisted: "I'm sure the FBI has the resources to investigate everybody."

Now I have drawn the following conclusions from my experiment: First, these self-described policing experts know absolutely nothing about police work. Any police investigation has to use known facts to narrow the scope of the inquiry, since manpower is finite. In this case, the FBI would be nuts *not* to use the nationalities and religious identities of the 19 hijackers to search for their co-conspirators among flight school alumni, since the hijackers themselves define their mission religiously.

Yet despite their obvious ignorance, the police critics in my canvas and others like them have controlled the public discourse about law enforcement for the last half decade, creating a public relations and policy nightmare for cops.

I also conclude from my experiment that if these critics exert the same influence over counterterrorism as they have over domestic policing—most significantly, through the anti-racial profiling movement of the 1990s—we're all in trouble. Indeed, we probably already missed an opportunity to avoid the terror of 9/11 because of their efforts.

Racial Profiling Is Justified

The debate around racial profiling is ultimately a debate about how to interpret numbers—specifically, the high stop and arrest rates of minorities. The people screaming about racial profiling hope to persuade the public that if the police stop and arrest proportionally more blacks than whites, for example, it's because officers are racist.

But there's obviously another possible explanation: Blacks are stopped and arrested more than whites because they commit more crime; racism has nothing to do with it.

To see how this debate plays out in practice, let's look at a beloved statistic of anti-police activists in New York. Blacks are 25 percent of New York City's population but are the subject of 50 percent of the stop-and-frisks conducted by the New York Police Department.

Now this statistic provides clear evidence of police bias, as the activists claim, only if all groups commit crime at equal rates.

But the facts are these: Blacks in New York are 13 times more likely to perpetrate a violent assault than whites, according to victim identifications of their assailants. Blacks commit about 62 percent of the assaults in New York City, so they are actually being frisked less than what their level of crime would predict.

Crime data and community complaints about crime, not racism, send the police to minority neighborhoods; once the police are deployed there, so-called racial profiling would be useless, because most people on the street are of the same race. Instead, the police look at suspicious behavior and location—a known

> *"A stereotype . . . is nothing more than a compilation of facts about who . . . attacked American interests in the past and who . . . is most likely to do so in the future."*

drug corner, say—in determining whom to stop. This is just good police work.

The result of the campaign against the police has been officer demoralization and unnecessarily strained police-community relations in minority neighborhoods. In those cities where the anti-police rhetoric has been particularly virulent, such as Cincinnati or Los Angeles, the cops have pulled back from discretionary activity, such as getting guns off the street. Crime has shot through the roof.

The Lack of Profiling Makes America Vulnerable

Unfortunately, it's not the ACLU [American Civil Liberties Union] that pays for police demoralization, it's the minority victims of crime. As I've discovered, there is a legion of law-abiding minority citizens in poor neighborhoods who see criminals, not the police, as the biggest threat in their lives, and who support law enforcement with all their hearts. The mainstream press, however, never seems to find them.

Now the exaggerations of contemporary police criticism would be bad enough if they only resulted in more domestic lawlessness. But I fear that they have also left us vulnerable to terrorist attacks.

In 1996, Vice President Al Gore chaired a commission on aviation security to strengthen airline defenses against terrorism. When word leaked out that the commission was considering a profiling system that would take into account a passenger's national origin and ethnicity, among other factors, in assessing the security risk he posed, the anti-law enforcement, as well as the Arab, lobby went ballistic. The counsel for the ACLU fired off an op-ed to the *Washington Post* complaining that "profiles select people who fit the stereotype of a terrorist. They frequently discriminate on the basis of race, religion, or national origin."

Now when the author invoked the terms "stereotype" and "discriminate," the reader was supposed to shriek in revulsion and march on the Federal Aviation Administration (FAA) in protest. But can we turn off our exquisitely honed racism radar for a moment and consider the question of terrorist profiles with cold reason? The ACLU's counsel complains that "profiles select people who fit the stereotype of a terrorist." But a stereotype in this case is nothing more than a compilation of facts about who has attacked American interests in the past and who, given what we know about the networks that promote anti-American terrorism, is most likely to do so in the future. It is [the terrorist group] al Qaeda and its brethren that have defined themselves by religion and regional interest, not American law enforcement.

Beyond mere numerical odds, there is no inherent connection between race and robbery. Whites may commit proportionally less robbery than blacks, but commit it they do. Islamic anti-American terrorism, on the other hand, is by its very definition perpetrated by Islamicists to avenge American imperialism in the Middle East. If we concentrate our investigation on Middle Eastern Muslims, we are not playing the odds, we are following the terrorists' own self-definition. We run virtually no risk of overlooking terrorists if our investigation ignores Unitarians from Minnesota, whereas, by contrast, the police will overlook robbers if they never consider whites as suspects.

Such hard truths about the terrorist threat, however, violate the central precept of our modern discourse about crime and law enforcement: that all groups commit crime, or, in this case, terrorism, at equal rates. So the Gore Commission dutifully abjured the inclusion of national origin, religion, ethnicity, and even gender in its recommended passenger profiling system. The result, the Computer-Assisted Passenger Profiling System, or CAPPS, omits precisely those criteria that are the major predictors of a predisposition to anti-American terrorism. Instead, CAPPS looks only at such behaviors as cash payments for tickets and one-way trips, behaviors which terrorists can easily change.

> *"It is irresponsible to argue that our severely limited resources for tracking down terrorists should be spread evenly across society."*

The anti-law enforcement ethos of the time further emasculated the terrorist-fighting potential of CAPPS. Because questioning or searching someone was now seen as akin to brutality—even, apparently, when performed by private security guards—the CAPPS system would be used only to secretly screen checked luggage; the owner of that luggage would not himself be searched, for that would be discriminatory.

Had a fully rational profiling system been put into place instead of CAPPS, one that takes advantage of everything we know about anti-American terrorism, there is a chance that the September 11 plot would have been foiled. As it was, two of the September 11 terrorists were flagged that day, presumably because of their travel itineraries and method of payment, but, consistent with the rules of the system, only their checked luggage was scrutinized. Had they themselves been searched, security officials may have wondered why two Arab men already under suspicion were carrying box-cutters, and looked further.

After the implementation of CAPPS, as the hijackers were learning to fly and casing their targets, the promoters of the equal crime and terrorism fiction busily kept up the pressure. Hussein Ibish of the Arab-American Anti-Discrimination Committee fumed in early 2000 that Americans were really hung up on this silly notion of Islamic terrorism. "Shadowy Arabs and Middle East terrorism fit into the mind of the media," he sneered. Of course an Algerian had just been caught with explosives to blow up the Los Angeles International Airport for the millennium, and Jordan had foiled other millennial plots against American interests in the Middle East. But we can't notice those facts, since doing so would contribute to stereotypes.

Islamic advocacy groups also incessantly complained about airport searches. The Department of Transportation penitentially ordered an audit of airline security checks, even though in all of 2000, only 15 Arab Americans actually filed discrimination complaints.

Audit Results Kept Secret

The results of that audit, performed last June [2002] at the Detroit Airport, remain a secret. It's not hard to guess why.

Let's assume that the audit shows that CAPPS still disproportionately selects people of Arabic ancestry, since it does flag passengers who have traveled frequently to terrorist-sponsoring states. Under the logic of the equal crime and terrorism fiction, the FAA would have to discard that travel criterion, since it is unacceptable that any group be shown to have a greater likelihood of terrorist associations than any other group. Before September 11, it is quite conceivable that the FAA would indeed have monkeyed with its passenger screening system until it created something that flags all groups equally. But after September 11, the FAA may be a little less willing to sacrifice safety for political correctness, so it is simply keeping the audit under wraps.

If the FAA is having second thoughts about the imperatives of the anti-law enforcement agenda, the primary keepers of that agenda have been totally unfazed by September 11.

I asked University of Toledo law professor David Harris, easily the loudest voice in the anti-racial profiling crusade, whether the New York police could rationally decide whether to focus their terrorism intelligence-gathering on mosques in Brooklyn or Catholic churches in Bensonhurst. "Why would I want to speculate on that?" he shot back, ducking the question.

I asked discrimination law professor Melissa Cole if there's an equal chance of a Scandinavian and Arab Islamic cell member. "I don't see why not," she said brightly. "Just because it's never happened before, doesn't mean [the Scandinavians] are not the next ones to commit a terrorist act."

This kind of radical skepticism may be fine for a freshman philosophy paper, but law professors should know better. It is irresponsible to argue that our severely limited resources for tracking down terrorists should be spread evenly across society.

There is a lesson to be drawn from our current predicament: bad ideas have consequences. We let them fester at our own risk.

As the campaign against the police gathered steam in the 1990s, few people spoke up against it, or tried to understand the complexities of policing that are suppressed in the anti-profiling crusade. Swearing opposition to racial profiling—and thereby implying its existence—became an easy way to show one's racial good faith, even if the swearer had not the slightest idea whether cops really practiced it. Now a construct that was bogus from the start is intruding itself into a battle even more serious than the war on crime.

Organizations to Contact

The editors have compiled the following list of organizations concerned with the issues debated in this book. The descriptions are derived from materials provided by the organizations. All have publications or information available for interested readers. The list was compiled on the date of publication of the present volume; the information provided here may change. Be aware that many organizations take several weeks or longer to respond to inquiries, so allow as much time as possible.

American Arab Anti-Discrimination Committee (ADC)
4201 Connecticut Ave. NW, Suite 300, Washington, DC 20008
(202) 244-2990 • fax: (202) 244-3196
e-mail: adc@adc.org • website: www.adc.org

The ADC is a civil rights organization committed to defending the rights of people of Arab descent and promoting their cultural heritage. It publishes a bimonthly newsletter, *ADC Times, Issue Papers* and *Special Reports*, which study key issues of defamation and discrimination; community studies, legal, media, and educational guides; and action alerts.

American Civil Liberties Union (ACLU)
125 Broad St., 18th Fl., New York, NY 10004-2400
(212) 549-2500
e-mail: aclu@aclu.org • website: www.aclu.org

The ACLU is a national organization that works to defend civil rights as guaranteed in the Constitution. It publishes various materials on civil liberties, including the triannual newsletter *Civil Liberties* and a set of handbooks on individual rights.

The ARC of the United States
1010 Wayne Ave., Suite 650, Silver Spring, MD 20910
(301) 565-3842 • fax: (301) 565-3843
e-mail: info@thearc.org • website: www.thearc.org

The ARC is the national organization of and for people with mental retardation and related developmental disabilities and their families. It is devoted to promoting and improving supports and services for people with mental retardation and their families. The association also fosters research and education regarding the prevention of mental retardation in infants and young children. The ARC publishes a variety of pamphlets and information sheets in English and Spanish. Most are available from the website.

Canadian Lesbian and Gay Archives
Box 639, Station A, Toronto, ON M5W 1G2 Canada
(416) 777-2755
website: www.clga.ca

The archives collects and maintains information and materials relating to the gay and lesbian rights movement in Canada and elsewhere. Its collection of records and other materials documenting the stories of lesbians and gay men and their organizations in

Canada is available to the public for the purpose of education and research. It also publishes an annual newsletter, *Lesbian and Gay Archivist.*

Cato Institute

1000 Massachusetts Ave. NW, Washington, DC 20001-5403
(202) 842-0200 • fax: (202) 842-3490
e-mail: cato@cato.org • website: http://cato.org

The institute is a libertarian public policy research foundation dedicated to limiting the role of government and protecting individual liberties. It is particularly concerned with the civil rights limitations of the USA Patriot Act. The institute publishes the quarterly magazine *Regulation*, the bimonthly *Cato Policy Report*, and numerous books and commentaries.

The Center for Public Integrity

910 Seventeenth St. NW, Seventh Fl., Washington, DC 20006
(202) 466-1300 • fax: (202) 466-1101
website: www.publicintegrity.org

The Center for Public Integrity works to provide the American people with the findings of investigations and analyses of public service, government accountability, and ethics-related issues. Publications include papers on the USA Patriot Act and possible creation of a USA Patriot II Act.

Human Rights Watch

350 Fifth Ave., 34th Fl., New York, NY 10118
(212) 290-4700
e-mail: hrwnyc@hrw.org • website: www.hrw.org

Human Rights Watch regularly investigates human rights abuses in over seventy countries around the world. It promotes civil liberties and defends freedom of thought, due process, and equal protection under the law. Its goal is to hold governments accountable for human rights violations they may commit against individuals because of their political, ethnic, or religious affiliations. It publishes the *Human Rights Watch* quarterly newsletter, the annual *Human Rights Watch World Report*, and a semiannual publications catalog.

Lambda Legal Defense and Education Fund, Inc.

666 Broadway, Suite 1200, New York, NY 10012
(212) 995-8585
website: www.lambdalegal.org

Lambda is a public-interest law firm committed to achieving full recognition of the civil rights of lesbians, gay men, and people with HIV/AIDs. The firm addresses a variety of areas, including equal marriage rights, the military, parenting and relationship issues, and domestic-partner benefits. It publishes the quarterly *Lambda Update* and the pamphlet *Freedom to Marry.*

Lawyers Committee for Human Rights (LCHR)

333 Seventh Ave., 13th Fl., New York, NY 10001-5004
(212) 845-5200 • fax: (212) 845-5299
e-mail: nyc@lchr.org • website: www.lchr.org

LCHR works in the United States and abroad to advance justice, human dignity, and respect for the rule of law. It supports human rights activists who fight for basic freedoms; protects refugees in flight from persecution and repression; promotes fair economic practices by safeguarding workers' rights; and helps build a strong international system of justice and accountability for human rights crimes. LCHR publishes reports and papers, including *A Year of Loss: Reexamining Civil Liberties Since September 11.*

National Association for the Advancement of Colored People (NAACP)
4605 Mt. Hope Dr., Baltimore, MD 21215
(877) NAACP-98
website: www.naacp.org

The primary focus of the NAACP continues to be the protection and enhancement of the civil rights of African Americans and other minorities. The NAACP works at the national, regional, and local level to secure civil rights through advocacy for supportive legislation and by the implementation of strategic initiatives. The organization publishes *Crisis*, a bimonthly magazine, and provides press releases on its website.

National Organization for Women (NOW)
733 Fifteenth St. NW, 2nd Fl., Washington, DC 20005
(202) 628-8669 • fax: (202) 785-8576
e-mail: now@now.org • website: www.now.org

The National Organization for Women is the largest organization of feminist activists in the United States. NOW's goal is to take action to bring about equality for all women. NOW works to promote affirmative action and eliminate discrimination and harassment in the workplace, schools, and justice system. The organization offers a quarterly publication, the *National NOW Times*, and publishes occasional reports and white papers.

People for the American Way Foundation (PFAW)
2000 M St. NW, Suite 400, Washington, DC 20036
(202) 467-4999 • fax: (202) 293-2672
e-mail: pfaw@pfaw.org • website: www.pfaw.org

PFAW works to increase tolerance and respect for America's diverse cultures, religions, and values. It distributes educational materials, leaflets, and brochures, including the reports *A Right Wing and a Prayer: The Religious Right in Your Public Schools* and *Attacks on the Freedom to Learn.*

Urban Institute
2100 M St. NW, Washington, DC 20037
(202) 261-5244
website: www.urban.org

The Urban Institute investigates social and economic problems confronting the nation and analyzes efforts to solve these problems. In addition, the institute works to improve government decisions and to increase citizen awareness about important public choices. It offers a wide variety of resources, including the report *Discrimination in Metropolitan Housing Markets.*

U.S. Department of Housing and Urban Development (HUD)
451 Seventh St. SW, Washington, DC 20410
(202) 708-1112
website: www.hud.gov

HUD's mission is to ensure a decent, safe, and sanitary home and suitable living environment for every American. In addition to creating opportunities for home ownership and providing housing assistance to low-income people, HUD is responsible for enforcing the nation's fair housing laws. It offers many resources, including the brochure *Fair Housing—It's Your Right!*

Bibliography

Books

William Kweku Asare	*Slavery Reparations in Perspective.* New Bern, NC: Trafford, 2003.
Carlos Ball	*The Morality of Gay Rights: An Exploration in Political Philosophy.* NewYork: Routledge, 2002.
Thomas C. Caramagno	*Irreconcilable Differences: Intellectual Stalemate in the Gay Rights Debate.* Westport, CT: Praeger, 2002.
Matt Cavanagh	*Against Equality of Opportunity.* New York: Clarendon Press, 2002.
Mitchell J. Chang et al.	*Compelling Interest: Examining the Evidence of Racial Dynamics in Colleges and Universities.* Palo Alto, CA: Stanford University Press, 2003.
James I. Charlton	*Nothing About Us Without Us: Disability Oppression and Empowerment.* Berkeley: University of California Press, 2000.
David Cole et al.	*Terrorism and the Constitution: Sacrificing Civil Liberties in the Name of National Security.* New York: New Press, 2002.
Richard Delgado	*Justice at War: Civil Liberties and Civil Rights During Times of Crisis.* New York: New York University Press, 2003.
Ingrid Gould Ellen	*Sharing America's Neighborhoods: The Prospect for Stable Integration.* Cambridge, MA: Harvard University Press, 2001.
Alphonse B. Ewing	*USA PATRIOT Act.* Hauppauge, NY: Nova Science, 2003.
Doris Zames Fleischer and Frieda Zames	*Disabilities Rights Movement: From Charity to Confrontation.* Philadelphia, PA: Temple University Press, 2001.
David A. Harris	*Profiles in Injustice: Why Racial Profiling Cannot Work.* New York: New Press, 2003.
David Horowitz	*Uncivil Wars: The Controversy over Reparations for Slavery.* San Francisco, CA: Encounter Books, 2003.
Dragon Milovanovic and Katheryn K. Russell, eds.	*Petit Apartheid in the U.S. Criminal Justice System: The Dark Figure of Racism.* Durham, NC: Carolina Academic Press, 2001.

179

Civil Rights

Stephen L. Ross and John Yinger	*The Color of Credit: Mortgage Discrimination, Research Methodology, and Fair-Lending Enforcement.* Cambridge, MA: MIT Press, 2002.
Stephen J. Schulhofer	*The Ememy Within: Intelligence Gathering, Law Enforcement, and Civil Liberties in the Wake of September 11.* New York: Twentieth Century Fund, 2002.
Mara S. Sidney	*Unfair Housing: How National Policy Shapes Community Action.* Lawrence: University Press of Kansas, 2003.
Anthony Stith	*Breaking the Glass Ceiling: Sexism and Racism in Corporate America: The Myths, Realities, and the Solutions.* Toronto: Warwick, 1998.
Raymond Winbush	*Should America Pay? Slavery and the Raging Debate on Reparations.* New York: Amistad Press, 2003.
Linda Wirth	*Breaking Through the Glass Ceiling: Women in Management.* Washington, DC: Brookings Institution, 2001.

Periodicals

Scotty Ballard	"How the Loss of Affirmative Action Could Affect You," *Jet*, April 21, 2003.
Anne Braden	"The Myth of Reverse Discrimination Revisited," *Peacework*, January 2000.
David Cole	"National Security State," *Nation*, December 17, 2001.
Victor Goode	"Crisis on Campus," *Colorlines*, Spring 2003.
Eric Hananoki	"It's Time for EDNA," *Democratic Underground*, January 17, 2002.
Robert L. Harris Jr.	"The Rise of the Black Middle Class," *World & I*, February 1999.
Jeff Johnson	"Controversial Anti-Terrorism Provisions Will Never Expire," July 8, 2002, www.cnsnews.com.
William Kiernan	"Where Are We Now: Perspectives on Employment of Persons with Mental Retardation," *Focus on Autism and Other Developmental Disabilities*, Summer 2000.
Brad Knickerbocker	"Affirmative Action's Unlikely Ally," *Christian Science Monitor*, October 25, 2000.
Beth Lemanowicz	"Mortgage Lending in Black, Brown, and White," *American Enterprise*, December 13, 2001.
Erik Lords	"Taking Sides," *Black Issues in Higher Education*, February 27, 2003.
Russell Madden	"Shattering the Glass Ceiling," March 12, 2000, www.home.earthlink.net.

Bibliography

Jeff Milchen	"War Is No Excuse to Surrender Hard-Won Civil Rights; It's Time to Do More than Complain," *Boulder Daily Camera*, July 8, 2003.
Kelly Patricia O'Meara	"Police State," *Insight on the News*, December 3, 2001.
Donna Payne	"Civil Rights, Gay Rights," *Advocate*, February 4, 2003.
Tony Pugh	"Hispanics Face More Housing Discrimination than Blacks," *Times Leader*, November 7, 2002.
Paul Schuck	"Affirmative Action: Don't Mend It or End It—Bend It," *Brookings Review*, Winter 2002.
Seattle Times	"Some Rights and Wrongs of Anti-Terrorism Laws," October 3, 2001.
Patricia Nell Warren	"Be Very Afraid—of Loss of Liberty at Home," *Gay and Lesbian Review Worldwide*, January/February 2002.
Peggy Whiteneck	"The Order of Merit," *Community College Week*, April 28, 2003.

Index